Beginning SSRS 2012 Joes 2 Pros®

A Tutorial for Beginners to Installing,
Configuring, and Formatting Reports using SQL
Server Reporting Services

By

Kathi Kellenberger

MS, MCSE: Data Platform

ISBN/EAN: 978-1-939666-21-5
Info@Joes2Pros.com

Table of Contents

3

About the Author

Kathi Kellenberger

After spending 16 years in a health care career she didn't love, Kathi Kellenberger decided it was time to follow her passion and turn a hobby into a new career as a Visual Basic programmer. As luck would have it, she eventually became a SQL Server database administrator in 2002 and finally found her niche.

On a whim, Kathi decided to write an article for her favorite web site, SQL Server Central, and before she knew what was happening, she had written a dozen articles for that site and two chapters of a SQL Server book. Her life has not been the same since, as she continues to share her passion about SQL Server by presenting at conferences and writing articles, blogs and books.

Acknowledgements from Kathi Kellenberger

They say that everything begins with a thought, an idea. After helping many people get started using Reporting Services, I had the great idea to turn what I had taught into a book. Luckily for me, Rick Morelan of Joes 2 Pros was looking for an author for an SSRS book. Thanks to Pinal Dave for introducing me to Rick. This is the first of, hopefully, many books originating from that meeting.

Writing a book is a big project. While the author gets most of the glory, it takes a small army of people to get the book into shape and in your hands. Thanks to Rick, Greg Lynch, Tony Smithlin, and anyone else who has contributed to making this book what it is today.

Thanks to Dennis for putting up with me while writing late into the night.

Dedication

To Elliott, may your life be full of fun and love.

Introduction

I first heard about SSRS at the 2003 PASS Summit (Professional Association for SQL Server). At that time, SQL Server 2000 was the latest version of SQL Server. SSRS was available as a free download, but in subsequent versions it was part of the regular installation media.

I knew that SSRS would help the IT department of the company where I worked. We didn't have a reporting tool in IT except for MS Access reports for our trouble ticket system and other systems. After I published the first reports, it wasn't long before word got around to other departments and I started receiving requests for reports outside of IT.

This was good news and bad. It was great that the managers in IT liked what I was doing, but I soon found myself overwhelmed with requests. Since I was the database administrator and had much more to do than create reports, I needed to come up with a solution. I realized that I had to get other people in the various departments to start developing reports and decided that I could teach them myself.

I ended up putting a short class together with just a slide deck and some labs, but I met the goal. Soon, several people were able to fill those requests, not just me. The best example was the HR department. They were already using Crystal Reports, but decided to switch to SSRS to save money and to get some extra functionality. They ended up converting all their reports by hand to SSRS over a few months.

After several opportunities to teach SSRS outside of my old company, I realized that I needed to be able to hand the students more than a slide deck. Even though SSRS is easy to learn, having a book to refer to can make a big difference when you are just getting started.

I finally decided I needed to write that book when I taught a combined T-SQL/SSRS class at my current company, Pragmatic Works. Pragmatic Works gave each of the students a copy of my Beginning T-SQL book but didn't have anything to give them that covered Reporting Services. I realized that I could take all that experience teaching SSRS and turn my knowledge into an inexpensive beginner book.

This book is the result of introducing dozens of people to SSRS. Enjoy!

About this Book

This book is meant to be a fantastic value that gets you started with SSRS. You will learn with many hands-on exercises that build on skills from chapter to chapter. Each chapter has a "Points to Ponder" section that summarizes the content, and you will also find a short review quiz at the end. We hope you enjoy this book. Please drop us a line and let us know how you like it or what you would like to learn next!

Skills Needed for this Book

SSRS stands for SQL Server Reporting Services. SSRS development is modeled after many Windows software products that allow you to add graphics and format text. Beyond that you only need to be able to turn on your computer, click a mouse, type a little and navigate to files and folders.

You should be able to install SQL Server on your computer. Your options are to search the Internet for a free download or buy a licensed copy. The official download site gets updated to a new location constantly. To get the most current installation steps go to www.Joes2Pros.com.

The preferred option is to get the Microsoft SQL Server 2012 Developer edition. The Joes 2 Pros site has a link to make this purchase. Microsoft offers a real bargain for students learning how to use SQL Server. For only $50 you can install and use the fully-enabled Developer edition as long as you agree to use it only for your own learning and to create your own code. This is an outstanding deal considering that businesses generally spend $10,000 to $100,000 to obtain and implement SQL Server Enterprise. More on these options and installation instructions can be found on the Joes2Pros.com web site.

.

Chapter 1.   Why SSRS?

Think of any invention in today's world that is widespread that everyone feels they need to use to make their work and home life function more efficiently. The most common thing that is probably coming to your mind is your car or other modern transportation. Before these inventions we had horses, sail boats, and could walk. With the combination of these techniques we could get to another city 200 miles away in a few days or go half way across the world in a few months.

With our more modern forms of transportation it takes only a few hours to get to the next major city, and we can get halfway across the world in less than 24 hours. You can cite time-saving and comfort as benefits. Flying first class to Sydney is likely more fun than how you would get there with the techniques used over a hundred years ago. Most of us know why and how we use today's widespread inventions and the value they offer us.

If you talk to an SSRS expert it's very clear to them exactly why companies really need this invention and how it saves time and adds business value. This short chapter will go into why SSRS is an important invention by showing how it improves the usage of information in your company. The rest of the book will show what SSRS is and how to use it.

The Need for a Reporting Tool

A friend of mine told me a story about doing database work in the 90s for a major company and how he wished SSRS was available back then. The Vice President of the marketing channel would often come to him just before an important meeting with the board of directors. He often needed to show how certain product sales were performing over time. All this information was in the database so it was my friend's job to get the information out and organized into a medium the VP could use. This medium was usually Excel. The VP often had meetings all over the world where he showcased this Excel report.

The solution to get the VP to him anywhere he was in the world was an Excel file attached to an e-mail. This worked pretty well but with some drawbacks. One time my friend sent the wrong file in the e-mail. A few minutes later my friend realized his mistake and sent another frantic e-mail to VP. This one was saying to ignore the last e-mail and use this newer one. Would the VP see the correct e-mail in time?

Then there were monthly meetings where the VP needed the same report with the most recent data. Time was spent re-running the queries and moving the data to Excel and updating the charts. The VP did say that no one should call in sick on the first day of the month or these reports would never get out. SSRS can solve this delivery and reuse problem very well.

Life without SSRS

Before SSRS there has always been a need for a company to benefit from the use of its own information. Excel spreadsheets have been a popular way to do this for a long time. With SSRS you can still use this solution and gain many other options too.

There was a solution to the frantic resent e-mail problem. The VP learned how to retrieve files from a network share location and just grab the latest file right before his meeting. There was another idea about creating an internal web site to host these reports but first we needed a budget to hire a web or SharePoint type of developer. Without SSRS it takes a team of many people to do what SSRS can do as on solution.

From these previous examples you can clearly see there has always been a need to get valuable information out of the data in your database. Necessity is the mother of invention so there are constant breakthroughs in making this easier, faster and even more impressive. SSRS is a big breakthrough in turning your data into valuable and welcomed information.

Life with SSRS

If SSRS had been available, my friend could have created a solution that let the VP run the report any time he wished. The report could have been published to the company intranet where the VP could run it from any of the offices he happened to be traveling to that month. There is a fair amount of work up front to develop and publish the report, but once that work is completed, the report can be reused as many times as needed. My friend could even be on vacation for the first day of the monthly and the VP can get his real-time report.

Not only could the report show the most recent data, the VP could choose to view reports of previous months with just a few clicks. The deployed SSRS is user friendly, and can also be configured to protect reports from being run by the wrong people.

You may be wondering if SSRS reports contain only words and numbers and you might be still dependent on Excel for charts. Luckily, SSRS has a rich set of visual components that add value and provide information with just a glance. This makes the reports look professional.

Life with SSRS is so much better for my friend, and can be for you, too!

[NOTES]

Chapter 2.   Meet SQL Server Reporting Services

Information is everywhere. But imagine the CIO of a company who has spent millions implementing databases and applications, yet doesn't know how to view that data in a way to make good decisions that make the company more profitable. That is where you come in. As a database professional you will be asked to provide answers to questions from the CIO and others in the company from that data. If your company is using SQL Server to host some of the company's data, chances are you will use SQL Server Reporting Services to create professional looking reports to hand to the CIO.

Benefits of SQL Server Reporting Services

At my first job as a database administrator, I was asked to look into a problem with some reports. Each manager in the department had his or her own version of an Access database with reports that were pointing to data in SQL Server. Even though the reports all started out the same, over time each manager had modified the definitions in his or her copy of the reports until they were no longer useful. None of the numbers were matching up.

Shortly after that, I found out that Microsoft was planning to release a web-based reporting tool called SQL Server Reporting Services that was free with SQL Server. Instead of trying to fix the problems in the existing reports, I could just start from scratch by creating the reports in Reporting Services. Now each manager would run the same reports each month…and get the same answers.

SQL Server Reporting Services (SSRS), a Business Intelligence component of SQL Server, is a feature-rich reporting tool. Reports can be published to a web page in the company intranet or even to SharePoint where the end users can run the reports whenever they wish.

READER NOTE: *In this book, you will publish reports to a web site called Report Manager. Integration with SharePoint is beyond the scope of this book.*

The person developing the report will design and preview the report on the computer. Once the report is complete, the developer will publish to Report Manager on the SSRS server. The end user can launch the report from Report Manager. Figure 2.1 illustrates the development, publishing and viewing of reports.

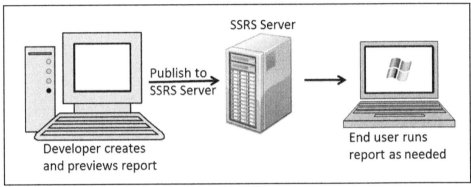

Figure 2.1 Develop, publish and run reports.

How to Install SSRS

You may not have the tools you need on your computer to build SSRS reports. For learning purposes, you can install everything you need on your personal laptop or desktop to develop and publish reports. The Developer Edition is recommended for following along in this book. If you plan to use the free Express edition be sure to download the Express with Advanced Services version.

Determine if SSRS is Installed

You may already have SSRS, or you may need to install it. Before doing any installation it makes sense to know where you are now. If you happened to install SQL Server with all features, you have the tools you need. There are two tools you need: SQL Server Data Tools and Reporting Services installed in Native Mode.

To find out if SQL Server Data Tools (SSDT) is installed, click the **Start** button, go to **All Programs**, and expand **SQL Server 2012**. Look for **SQL Server Data Tools** (Figure 2.2).

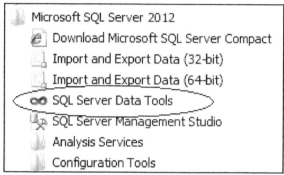

Figure 2.2 Navigation to SQL Server Data Tools.

Now, let's check to see if SQL Server Reporting Services is installed. Click the **Start** > **All Programs** > **SQL Server 2012** > **Configuration Tools** > **SQL** > **Server Configuration Manager** (Figure 2.3).

Figure 2.3 SQL Server Configuration Manager.

Once Configuration Manager is running, select **SQL Server Services**. Look for **SQL Server Reporting Services** in the list of services installed (Figure 2.4). If you have both SQL Server Reporting Services service and SQL Server Developer tools installed, you will not have to install them again. In that case skip to the Configure Reporting Services section.

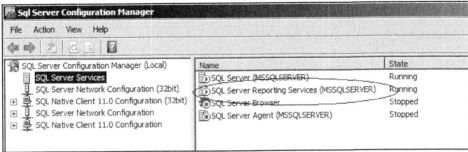

Figure 2.4 Configuration Manager shows all SQL Server Services.

Install SQL Server Data Tools and Report Manager

I am assuming you know how to start a SQL Server 2012 installation. If not you can watch the video at www.Joes2Pros.com for a video tutorial. This book will use the term "Double-click the SQL Server 2012 installation media" but if you have the DVD in hand then it may mean you just need to place that into your drive to begin the installation media.

If you have installed SQL Server, but are missing the Data Tools or Reporting Services, follow these instructions:

Double-click the SQL Server 2012 installation media. Click the Installation link on the left (Figure 2.5) to view the Installation options. Click the top link **New SQL Server stand-alone installation or add features to an existing installation**.

Figure 2.5 SQL Server Installation Center.

Follow the SQL Server Setup wizard until you get to the Installation Type screen. At that screen, select **Add features to an existing instance of SQL Server 2012**. Click **Next** to move to the **Feature Selection** page. Select **Reporting Services – Native** and **SQL Server Data Tools** (Figure 2.6). If the **Management Tools** have not been installed, go ahead and choose them as well.

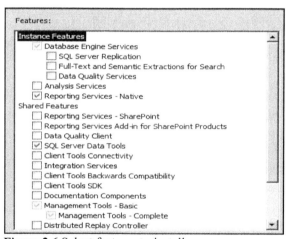

Figure 2.6 Select features to install.

Continue through the wizard and reboot the computer at the end of the installation if instructed to do so.

Configure Reporting Services

If you installed Reporting Services during the installation of the SQL Server instance, SSRS will be configured automatically for you. If you

18

install SSRS later, then you will have to go back and configure it as a subsequent step.

Click **Start** > **All Programs** > **Microsoft SQL Server 2012** > **Configuration Tools** > **Reporting Services Configuration Manager** > **Connect** on the Reporting Services Configuration Connection dialog box (Figure 2.7).

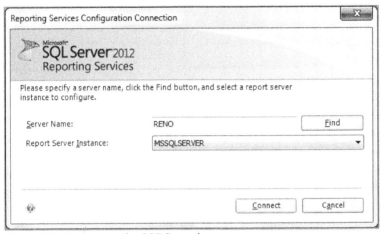

Figure 2.7 Connect to the SSRS service.

On the left-hand side of the Reporting Services Configuration Manager, click **Database** (Figure 2.8). Click the **Change Database** button on the right side of the screen.

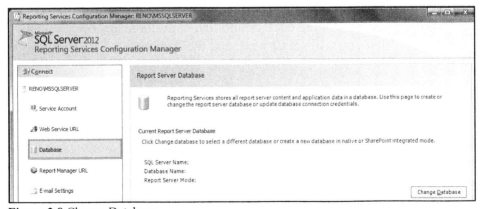

Figure 2.8 Choose Database.

19

Select **Create a new report server database** (Figure 2.9) and click **Next**.

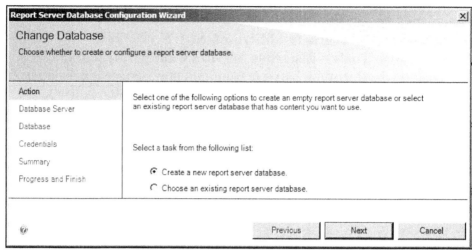

Figure 2.9 Create a new report server database.

Click through the rest of the wizard accepting the defaults. This wizard creates two databases: ReportServer, used to store report definitions and security, and ReportServerTempDB which is used as scratch space when preparing reports for user requests.

Now click **Web Service URL** (Figure 2.10) on the left-hand side of the Reporting Services Configuration Manager. Click the **Apply** button to accept the defaults. If the **Apply** button has been grayed out, move on to the next step. This step sets up the SSRS web service. The web service is the program that runs in the background that communicates between the web page, which you will set up next, and the databases.

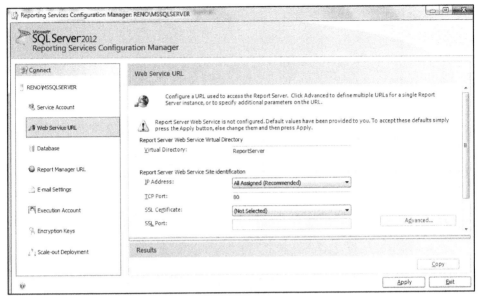

Figure 2.10 Choose Web Service URL.

The final configuration step is to select the **Report Manager URL** (Figure 2.11) link on the left. Accept the default settings and click **Apply**. If the **Apply** button was already grayed out, this means the SSRS was already configured. This step sets up the Report Manager web site where you will publish reports. You may be wondering if you also must install a web server on your computer. SQL Server does not require that the Internet Information Server (IIS), the Microsoft web server, be installed to run Report Manager.

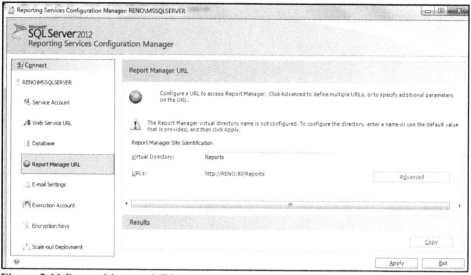

Figure 2.11 Report Manager URL.

Click **Exit** to dismiss the Reporting Services Configuration Manager dialog box.

What You Can Do with SSRS

You have SSRS installed and configured, but you still may not be convinced that it is the reporting tool for you. Just like buying a car, you want to take a test drive first, so now you will get the chance to see an actual report.

Make sure you have downloaded and installed the sample code and projects from the Joes 2 Pros web site to C:\Joes2Pros\SSRSCompanionFiles. You must also have installed SQL Server Data Tools (SSDT) on your computer. The installation for SSDT is described in the "Install SQL Server Data Tools and Report Manager" section earlier in this chapter.

Navigate to C:\Joes2Pros\SSRSCompanionFiles\Chapter2\Solution\ and double-click the Joes2Pros.sln file. After a minute or so, SSDT will launch. The very first time that you launch SSDT, it will ask you for a setting preference. Choose the **Business Intelligence** setting. SSDT is actually part of Visual Studio. If you have done any programming in Visual Basic or C#, you will recognize this tool. If not, don't worry, I'll provide plenty of help to get you around in SSDT.

For right now, you will just take a look at an actual report. On the right-hand side of the screen, you should see a window called Solution Explorer (Figure 2.12).

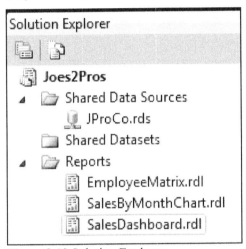

Figure 2.12 Solution Explorer.

*READER NOTE: If you do not see the Solution Explorer, from the menu select **Window** > **Reset Window Layout**. When asked if you really want to do this, click **Yes**. It is very easy to mess up the windows in SSDT, so remember this little trick in case you need to use it later.*

In the Solution Explorer, there are three reports. Double-click the **SalesDashboard.rdl** report. The report will display in Design view in the middle of the screen (Figure 2.13).

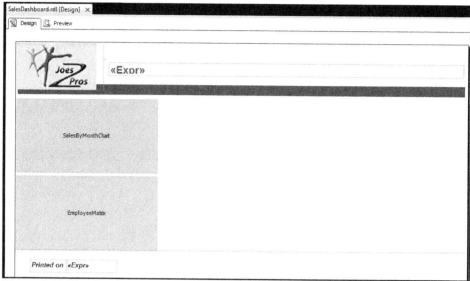

Figure 2.13 Viewing the report in Design view.

In this view of your report, notice there are two tabs. One is called Design and the other is called Preview. Try launching the report by clicking **Preview**.

READER NOTE: If you did not install SQL Server as a default instance, you will need to modify the Data Source before you can see the report. You will learn how to do this in Chapter 4.

You should see the report displayed with data from 2012 (Figure 2.14). You can select a different year from the dropdown list and click **View Report** to see data from different years. Expand the Categories to see the totals broken down by month. Hover the mouse over the charts to see the actual sales totals.

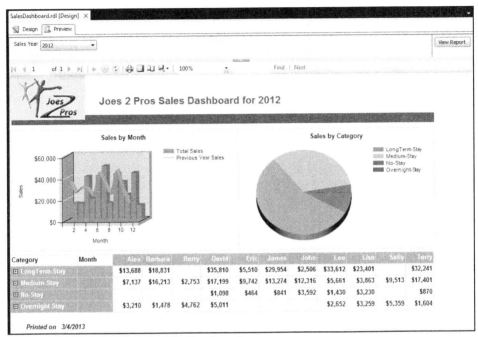

Figure 2.14 Viewing the report in Preview view.

Notice the report has some nice looking charts at the top and something at the bottom that looks like a spreadsheet with a grid of data. The grid of data is often either a table or a matrix. This report uses a matrix but the exact meaning of that term you will learn about later in the book. For right now when you hear the term Matrix or Table just think of a grid of data showing on your report.

You can add many visual elements to reports, and this dashboard just displays a small sample of what is possible. You can add charts and gauges into report cells and you can even add maps.

Summary

SSRS, a component of SQL Server, is a feature-rich reporting tool. You can develop professional and informative reports that the end users in your company can view whenever they desire.

All of the tools you need to learn report development and publishing can easily be installed on your personal laptop or desktop computer. You will use SQL Server Data Tools to create and edit reports. After publishing the report to Reporting Services, you can view the reports from Report Manager, the SSRS web site.

Points to Ponder – Meet SQL Server Reporting Services

1.   SQL Server Reporting Services (SSRS) comes with SQL Server.

2.   You can use SSRS to create reports.

3.   The reports can be viewed on your own computer or shared with others in your organization.

4.   You can create tabular and matrix reports.

5.   A matrix report is pivoted – some of the data has been changed into column headings. For example, the months of the year might be column headings.

6.   You can create reports with visual elements such as charts and maps.

7.   To get the tool to create reports, you must select SQL Server Data Tools when installing SQL Server.

8.   SQL Server Data Tools is an add-in for Visual Studio.

9.   If your windows inside SSDT get messed up, set them back to the default by Windows >Reset Window Layout.

10.   A project in SSDT can contain one or more reports.

11.   To get the SSRS Report Manager web site, install SQL Server Reporting Services – Native Mode when installing SQL Server.

12.   Reporting Services can be installed natively or to SharePoint (you will do native mode).

13.   Even though SSRS reports can be deployed to a web site, IIS (a web server) is not required.

Review Quiz – Chapter Two

1) Which types of elements can be added to Reporting Services reports?

  O a. Tabular reports
  O b. Matrix reports
  O c. Charts
  O d. All of the above

2) Which statement is false?

  O a. A web server (IIS) is required for Report Manager.
  O b. Reporting Services is a component of SQL Server.
  O c. You can preview the report you are designing within SSDT.
  O d. End users can view reports from Report Manager.

Answer Key

1) There are several types of reports that you can build with SSRS including tabular, matrix, charts, maps and more. All of the above, (d), is the correct answer.

2) All of the statements are true except for (a), making it the right answer. Even though SSRS reports are published to a web site, Report Manager, a web server (IIS) is not required.

[NOTES]

Chapter 3.   Your First Report

In today's world automation is all around you. Henry Ford began building his Model T automobiles on a moving assembly line a century ago and changed the world. The moving assembly line allowed Ford to build identical cars quickly and cheaply. Henry Ford said in his autobiography "Any customer can have a car painted any colour that he wants so long as it is black."

Today you can buy a car straight from the factory with your choice of several colors and with many options like back up cameras, built-in navigation systems and heated leather seats. The assembly lines now use robots to perform some tasks along with human workers. When you order your new car, if you want something special, not offered by the manufacturer, you will have to find a way to add it later.

In computer software, we also have "assembly lines" called wizards. A wizard will ask you a series of questions, often branching to specific questions based on earlier answers, until you get to the end of the wizard. These wizards are used for many things, from something simple like setting up a rule in Outlook to performing administrative tasks on a server.

Often, a wizard will get you part of the way to the end result, enough to get much of the tedious work out of the way. Once you get the product from the wizard, if the wizard is not capable of doing something you need, you can tweak the results.

In this chapter, you will build a report the easy way – with a wizard. Then you will get the chance to spruce the report up a bit.

Create a Report with the Report Wizard

Let's get started with your first report!

Launch SQL Server Data Tools (SSDT) from the Start menu under SQL Server 2012. Once SSDT is running, click **New Project** to launch the New

Project dialog box. On the left side of the screen expand **Business Intelligence** and select **Reporting Services**. Configure the properties as shown in Figure 3.1. Be sure to select **Report Server Project Wizard** as the type of report and to save the project in the C:\Joes2Pros\SSRSCompanionFiles\Chapter3\Project folder.

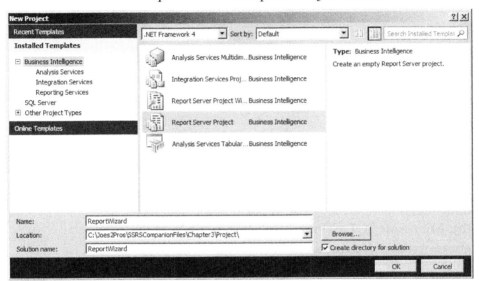

Figure 3.1 The New Project dialog box.

Click **OK** and wait for the Report Wizard to launch. Click **Next** on the Welcome screen (Figure 3.2).

Figure 3.2 The Welcome screen.

On the Select the Data Source screen (Figure 3.3), make sure that **New data source** is selected. Type **JProCo** as the data source name. Make sure that **Microsoft SQL Server** is selected in the Type dropdown.

Figure 3.3 Select the data source.

Click **Edit** to configure the connection string on the Connection Properties dialog box. If your SQL Server database server is installed on your local computer, type in **localhost** for the Server name and select the **JProCo** database from the **Select or enter a database name** dropdown (Figure 3.4).

Figure 3.4 Configure the connection properties.

READER NOTE: If you installed a named instance of SQL Server, you will have to specify the fully qualified name, i.e., SERVER_NAME\INSTANCE_NAME. For example, an instance named SQL2012 on the local machine would be Localhost\SQL2012. If you installed SQL Server Express then it would be called Localhost\SQLExpress.

Click **OK** to dismiss the Connection Properties dialog box. Check **Make this a shared data source** and click **Next**.

On the Design the Query screen, you can use the query builder to build a query if you wish. Since this book is not meant to teach you T-SQL queries, you will copy all queries from files that have been provided for you. In the C:\Joes2Pros\SSRSCompanionFiles\Chapter3\Resources folder open the **sales by employee.sql** file. Copy and paste the code from the file into the **Query string** Text Box (Figure 3.5). Click **Next**.

Figure 3.5 The query.

On the Select the Report Type screen, choose **Tabular** (Figure 3.6) and click **Next**.

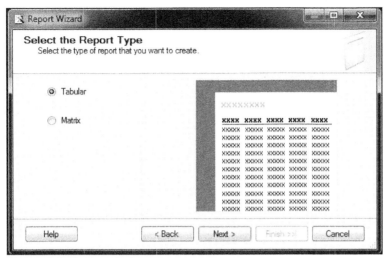

Figure 3.6 Choose tabular.

On the Design the Table screen, you have to figure out the groupings of the report. How do you do this? Well, you often need to know a bit about the data and report requirements. I often draw the report out on paper first to help me determine the groups.

In the case of this report, I could group the data several ways. Do I want to see the data grouped by Year and Month? Do I want to see the data grouped by Employee or Category? The only thing I know for sure about this ahead of time is that the TotalSales goes in the Details section. Let's assume that the CIO asked to see the data grouped first by Year and Month, then by Category.

Let's move the fields to the right-hand side. This is done by selecting **Page > Group** or **Details >**, as shown in Figure 3.7, and click **Next**.

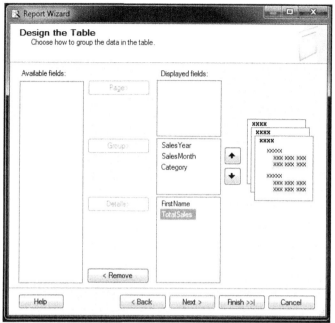

Figure 3.7 Design the Table.

On the Choose the Table Layout screen, select **Stepped** and check **Include subtotals** and **Enable drilldown**, as shown in Figure 3.8.

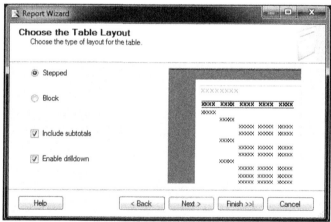

Figure 3.8 The table layout.

On the Choose the Style screen, choose any color scheme you wish (unlike the Model T) and click **Next**. I chose the default, Slate. On the Choose the Deployment Location screen, change the Deployment folder to **Chapter 3** (Figure 3.9) and click **Next**.

READER NOTE: The location settings may or may not be correct depending on how you installed SSRS. You will take another look at these settings when you learn about deployment in Chapter10.

Figure 3.9 The deployment properties.

At the Completing the Wizard screen, name your report **Employee Sales** (Figure 3.10) and click **Finish**.

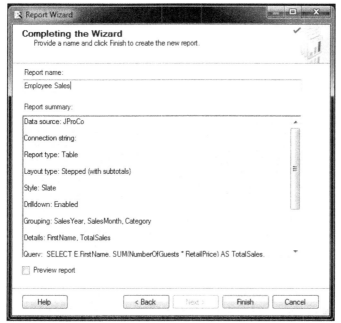

Figure 3.10 Complete the wizard.

After clicking **Finish**, the report and a shared data source will appear in the Solution Explorer and the report will also be visible in Design view (Figure 3.11).

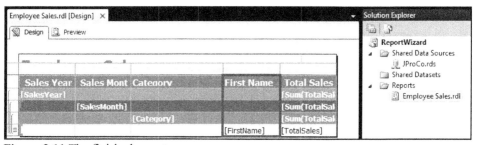

Figure 3.11 The finished report.

Click the **Preview** tab at the top. This report expects the user to supply a year which the report will then use as a filter. Type in a year between 2006 and 2013 and click **View Report** (Figure 3.12).

Figure 3.12 Click the Preview tab.

Click the plus sign next to the Sales Year to expand the report to see the months, then expand again to see the categories and finally the details (Figure 3.13).

Employee Sales

Sales Year	Sales Month	Category	First Name	Total Sales
2007				351830.6804
	1			27136.7714
		LongTerm-Stay		1640.7300
			Lee	1640.7300
		Medium-Stay		11597.4760
		No-Stay		2547.2380
		Overnight-Stay		11351.3274
	2			10489.9566
	3			48552.0600
	4			26146.6304
	5			51526.1562
	6			33974.0464
	7			33021.3890
	8			20036.1450
	9			25551.6802
	10			31870.1916
	11			25173.1216
	12			18352.5320

Figure 3.13 The expanded report.

You now have the assembly line report completed, and you probably already have some ideas on how to improve the report.

Spruce up the "ReportWizard" Report

The report looks pretty good and you know these numbers represent money. If that is the case, the report doesn't need to use four decimal points. Simple dollars will work just fine. The left side of Figure 3.14 shows our existing report and on the very right-hand side is our goal for the Total Sales field. This field should appear as currency with no decimal points.

rst Name	Total Sales	Name	Total Sales
	314645.0804		$314,645
	31168.6684		$31,169
	17814.3170		$17,814
	24258.5742		$24,259
	27865.1878		$27,865
	11955.8384		$11,956
	14776.6302		$14,777
	44133.9692		$44,134
	13815.1620		$13,815
	34202.7824		$34,203
	41345.2390		$41,345
	40353.0256		$40,353
	12955.6862		$12,956

Figure 3.14 Total sales before and after formatting.

Click the **Design** tab to go back to Design view. You will modify the report by selecting report cells and modifying the properties, but there is a trick to selecting those cells. You can select a cell by clicking it, but you can also select the contents of the cell instead. The best technique I have found to select the cell itself is to click right at the edge of the cell. Figure 3.15 shows a selected cell. Notice that there is a dark outline around the cell. Figure 3.16 shows the contents of a cell selected. The inside of the cell has changed color.

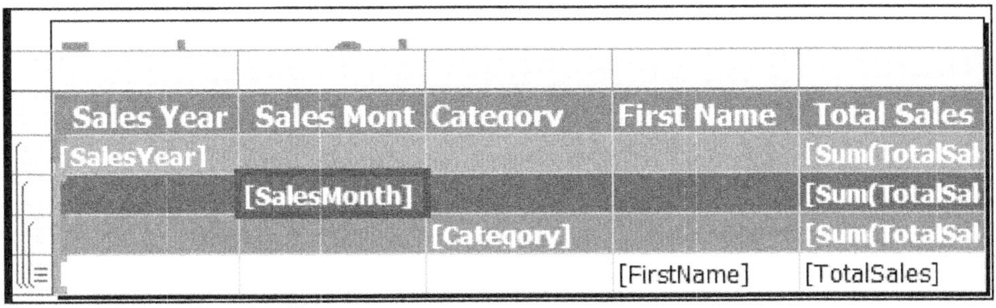

Figure 3.15 A selected cell.

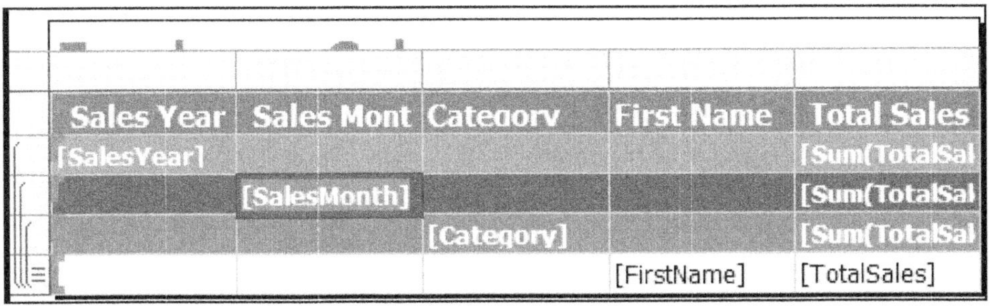

Figure 3.16 Selected contents of a cell.

You will also see when selecting a cell that a list of available fields will display. This is very handy when designing a report from scratch or when you need to change the contents of the cell to a different field. Another thing you can do is right-click the cell to get a menu of actions to perform. I have had the best luck by just hovering over the cell and then right-clicking.

The first thing you will do is to change the format of all cells below the Total Sales heading to currency. Right-click one of the cells and choose **Text Box Properties**. This brings up the Text Box Properties dialog box. Select **Number** on the left and then choose **Currency** under the Category. Change the **Decimal places** to **0** and check **Use 1000 separator**. The dialog box should look like Figure 3.17. Click **OK**.

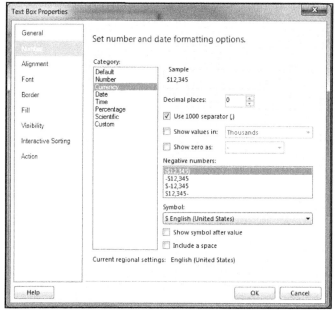

Figure 3.17 The Text Box Properties.

READER NOTE: *My settings are set up for United States currency; your settings may be for a different country.*

Repeat this process for each of the cells below the Total Sales header. The next thing to change is to increase the width of the Category column. Whenever any of the cells are selected, the table handles are visible. Click the gray cell, called a column handle, above the Category heading to select the column, as shown in Figure 3.18.

Sales Year	Sales Mont	Category	First Name	Total Sales
[SalesYear]				[Sum(TotalSal
	[SalesMonth]			[Sum(TotalSal
		[Category]		[Sum(TotalSal
			[FirstName]	[TotalSales]

Figure 3.18 Select the Category column.

Hover your mouse pointer over the right edge of the gray handle above Category and then drag the edge to the right increasing the size by about double. Now preview the report again, remembering to enter a year and to expand the sections to see the changes (Figure 3.19).

Year	2007

◄ ◄ 1 of 1 ► ►◄				100%	▾

Employee Sales

Sales Year	Sales Month	Category		First Name	Total Sales
⊟ 2007					$351,831
	⊟ 1				$27,137
		⊟ LongTerm-Stay			$1,641
				Lee	$1,641
		⊟ Medium-Stay			$11,597
				Barbara	$4,796
				Sally	$6,801
		⊞ No-Stay			$2,547
		⊞ Overnight-Stay			$11,351
	⊞ 2				$10,490
	⊞ 3				$48,552

Figure 3.19 The updated report.

Summary

The Report Wizard is a great tool to get you started authoring reports with SSRS. The wizard creates a pretty nice report that is *almost* good enough to hand to the CEO or CIO. Like many things created with automation, you will want to spend some time cleaning up the formatting.

Points to Ponder – Your First Report

1. You can use a wizard to easily create a report.

2. The wizard can create reports with features such as grouping levels, matrix reports and expanding sections.

3. You will probably have to tweak the report you create with the wizard, such as cleaning up the formatting.

4. The formats of rows, columns and cells can be changed.

5. You can change a cell to display as currency.

6. Configure properties of cells by right-clicking objects and choosing Properties.

7. To select the cell, click the edge of the cell.

8. To select the contents of a cell, click into the cell.

9. You can preview the reports inside SSDT.

10. Reports will be found in the Solution Explorer.

Review Quiz – Chapter Three

1) Which statement is true about the Report Wizard?

  O a. The Report Wizard produces a report that is not very useful. You should avoid it.

  O b. You must use the Query Builder when creating a report with the Report Wizard.

  O c. Once running the Report Wizard, you cannot modify any of the report properties such as formatting.

  O d. The Report Wizard gives you the choice of creating a Tabular or Matrix report.

2) Where will you find the report after creating it?

  O a. In the Solution Explorer.

  O b. In the Solution Folder.

  O c. In the Report Explorer

Answer Key

1) The Report Wizard produces a report that is pretty good so (a) is wrong. You can tweak the final report to modify the formatting and other properties so (c) is wrong. While running the report, you can make several choices; one of those choices is whether to have a Tabular or Matrix report making answer (a) false. The correct answer is (d) since you can create a Tabular or Matrix report with the Wizard.

2) You will find the final report in the Solution Explorer , answer (a).

[NOTES]

Chapter 4.   Connect to Your Data

When I was a child, the telephone book was an important part of my life. Maybe I was just a nerd, but I enjoyed getting a new book every year to page through to learn about the businesses in my small town or to discover where some of my school acquaintances lived. It was also the source of maps to my town's neighborhoods and the towns that surrounded me.

To make a phone call, I would need a telephone number. In order to find a telephone number, I had to know how to use the telephone book. That seems pretty simple, but it resembles connecting to any data. You have to know where the data is and how to interact with it.

Creating a Shared Data Source

A data source is the connection information that the report uses to connect to the database. You have two choices when creating a data source, whether to embed it in the report or to make it a shared resource usable by many reports.

The best advice I can give you is to create shared data sources. The reason I recommend this is that if a database moves to a new server you will have just one place in Report Manager to make the server name change. That one change will update the connection information in all the reports that use that data source.

To get started, you will start with a fresh project. Go to **Start** > **All Programs** > **SQL Server 2012** > **Microsoft SQL Server Data Tools** to launch SSDT. Once SSDT is running, click **New Project** to create a new project. Once the New Project dialog box appears, fill in the form, as shown in Figure 4.1. Be sure to select **Report Server Project** this time – not the wizard.

Figure 4.1 Choose the Report Server Project.

Click **OK** to dismiss the New Project dialog box. You should now have an empty project, as shown in the Solution Explorer (Figure 4.2).

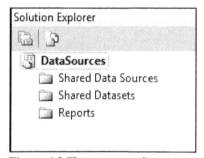

Figure 4.2 The empty project.

A report is meant to show you data. Where is the data? The first task is to create a Shared Data Source. Right-click on the **Shared Data Sources** folder and choose **Add New Data Source** (Figure 4.3).

Figure 4.3 Add new data source.

The Shared Data Source Properties dialog box will launch where you can fill in a name for the data source. By default, it is named DataSource1. The best practice is to give the data source a more meaningful name. It is possible that you will have projects with more than one data source and, by naming them, you can tell one from another. Type the name **JProCo** for the data source name and click the **Edit** button to configure the database connection properties.

You'll use SQL Server primarily for data throughout this book. If you take a look at the types of data sources you can choose, you will see that SSRS works with many data platforms including Oracle, XML, and Teradata. Make sure **SQL Server** is selected before continuing.

For this book, I am assuming that you are using a local SQL Server and that you can use your Windows account to log in to the SQL Server. If, for some reason you must use **SQL Server Authentication**, choose that option and fill in your SQL Server account credentials. Otherwise, just accept **Windows Authentication**.

If you followed along in Chapter 3, this should look familiar. If your database server was installed locally and with the default instance, just type in **Localhost** for the Server name. Select the **JProCo** database from the database list. At this point, the connection properties should look like Figure 4.4.

Figure 4.4 Connection Properties.

If you have installed a named instance of SQL Server, you will have to specify the server name like this: Localhost\InstanceName, replacing the InstanceName with whatever your instance name is. If you are not sure about the named instance, launch the SQL Server Configuration Manager (Figure 4.5) found at **Start > All Programs > Microsoft SQL Server 2012 > Configuration Tools**. If you have a named instance, the name will be shown in parentheses. A default instance of SQL Server will display MSSQLSERVER; a named instance will display the name chosen during installation.

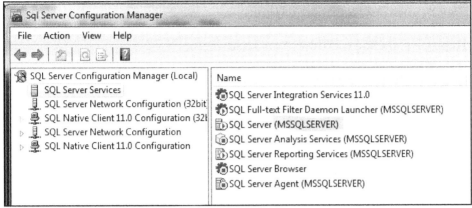

Figure 4.5 Default or named instance.

Once you get the connection properties filled in, click **OK** to dismiss the Connection Properties dialog box and **OK** again to dismiss the **Shared Data Source** properties. You now have a data source in the Solution Explorer (Figure 4.6).

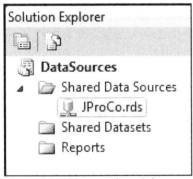

Figure 4.6 The new shared data source.

*READER NOTE: You can get to the properties of just about anything in SSRS by right-clicking and choosing **Properties**. The exception is the Shared Data Source. When you right-click and choose **Properties**, a Properties window opens that just shows the location of a file. To actually modify the data source, double-click it instead.*

You won't develop an entire report during this chapter, but you do need to create one just to learn how to work with the data source. Right-click on **Reports** and choose **Add > New Item** (Figure 4.7).

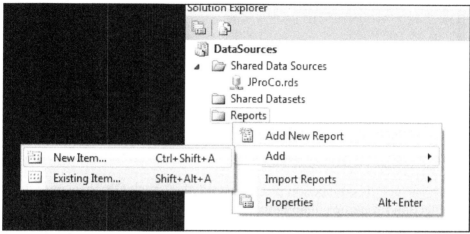

Figure 4.7 Choose New Item.

Be sure not to select the **Add New Report** item. That choice actually launches the Report Wizard. In this case, you just need a blank report. Once you select **New Item**, the Add New Item dialog box launches. At this point, you can choose from several items including the Report Wizard, as shown in Figure 4.8.

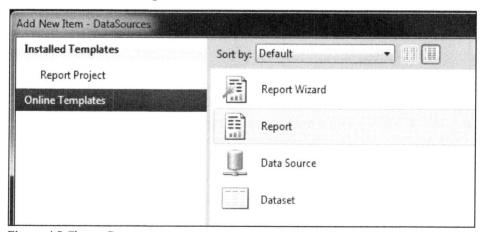

Figure 4.8 Choose Report.

Select **Report**, change the Name of the report to **Data Source Example.rdl** (Figure 4.9) and click **Add**.

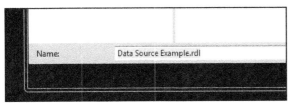

Figure 4.9 Name the report.

Now that you have a new blank report in place, you should see the Report Data window on the left side of the screen. If you do not see it, click **CTRL + ALT + D** to display the window (Figure 4.10).

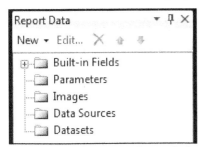

Figure 4.10 The Report Data window.

Even though the shared data source has been created, you will need to create a data source inside the report that points to the shared data source. Right-click the **Data Sources** folder in the Report Data window and choose **Add Data Source** (Figure 4.11).

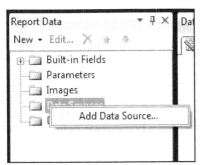

Figure 4.11 Add Data Source.

53

Clicking **Add Data Source** launches the Data Source Properties window. Type **JProCo** as the Name. Select **Use shared data source reference** and select **JProCo** from the dropdown list. The form should look like Figure 4.12.

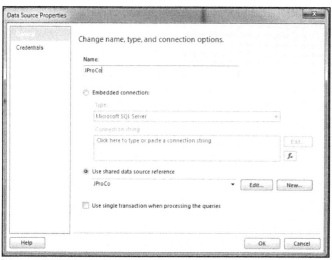

Figure 4.12 The Data Source Properties.

Click **OK** and now you should see the report's data source in the Report Data window (Figure 4.13). Notice the little arrow that signifies that the data source points to the shared data source.

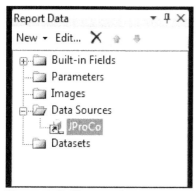

Figure 4.13 The new data source.

The data source is now in place, and you will use it to create a dataset next.

Creating a Dataset

Make sure you have followed the steps in the Creating a Shared Data Source section before beginning this section. If the **DataSources** project is not open, navigate to C:\Joes2Pros\SSRSCompanionFiles\Chapter4\Projects\DataSources\ and double-click the **DataSources.sln** file.

Right-click the **Datasets** folder and choose **Add Dataset**, as shown in Figure 4.14.

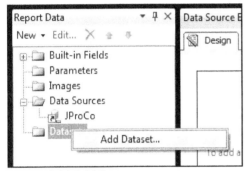

Figure 4.14 Add Dataset.

Once you select **Add Dataset**, the Dataset Properties dialog box opens. Just like the data sources, it is a good practice to name all of your datasets with a meaningful name. Name this one **EmployeeSales.** Select **Use a dataset embeded in my report** and select **JProCo** from the Data Source dropdown list.

READER NOTE: You may be wondering why you won't use a shared dataset instead. Most of the time, a dataset will be embeded in the report because the query will be unique to that report and not reused. Shared datasets are great for data that is used in many places, such as parameter lists that give the user a list of values to choose from when they run the report.

Make sure that **Text** is selected under **Query Type**. You can also create the query by using the Query Designer or creating a stored procedure in SQL Server. A stored procedure is a saved script that can return data to applications or reporting tools.

Since this book is not meant to teach you T-SQL, you will get all of the queries from text files and not attempt to type them. Find the **sales by employee.sql** file located in the C:\Joes2Pros\SSRSCompanionFiles\Chapter4\Resources folder. Copy and paste the text found in that file into the **Query** text box or click **Import** and navigate to the file. The dialog box should look like Figure 4.15.

Figure 4.15 The dataset properties.

Click **OK**, and now you should see the dataset for the report along with all the fields you will use to build the report (Figure 4.16).

Figure 4.16 The new dataset.

Testing the Dataset

Now that you have created a dataset, you may be wondering just what to do with it. The dataset is the query behind your report. Make sure the Toolbox is open. If not, type **CTRL + ALT + X**. To see the dataset in action, drag a **Table** control from the **Toolbox** onto the report design surface. The table will look like Figure 4.7.

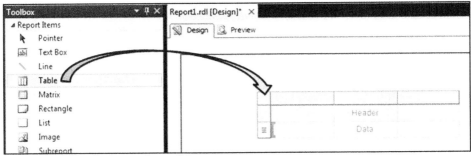

Figure 4.17 The design surface of the report.

From the dataset you just created, drag the **FirstName** field to the first cell in the Data row. Drag the **Category** field to the next cell of the Data row.

Drag the **SalesYear** field to the third cell in the Data row. The report should look like Figure 4.18. Notice how SSRS added the field names to the Header row automatically and added spaces to the names.

First Name	Category	Sales Year
[FirstName]	[Category]	[SalesYear]

Figure 4.18 The table grid with fields.

Add a fourth column to the report by right-clicking the **Sales Year** column and selecting **Insert Column > Right**. Repeat to add one more column. This time, hover your cursor over the blank data cell until you see a small icon appear. This icon is a list of possible fields from the dataset. Select **SalesMonth** for the fourth Data cell. Select **TotalSales** for the fifth Data cell. You will often find there is more than one way to perform just about any task in SSRS. Figure 4.19 shows the final table.

First Name	Category	Sales Year	Sales Month	Total Sales
[FirstName]	[Category]	[SalesYear]	[SalesMonth]	[TotalSales]

Figure 4.19 Final table.

Click **Preview** to view the report and enter the year **2006**. Click **View Report**. Obviously, this report is not ready to hand to your boss, but it does illustrate how the dataset actually works.

Other Data Sources

In a perfect world, all data would be stored in SQL Server. Since most companies are in the real world, not a perfect one, data may be stored in alternate database systems, Excel spreadsheets, text documents and more. Luckily, SSRS is compatible with data from many different database systems. Microsoft supplies drivers that communicate between its products and most types of data sources. To demonstrate, you will create a report that pulls the data from an Excel spreadsheet. The standard for communicating between systems is called ODBC which stands for Open

Database Connectivity. Any system that is ODBC compatible will work with SSRS in addition to the dedicated drivers for systems like Oracle.

To connect SSRS to an Excel spreadsheet, you will have to set up an ODBC data source. There are two ways to do this. From the **Search programs and files box** in the **Windows Start** menu, type c:\windows\sysWOW64\odbcad32.exe. This launches a dialog box that will let you create a link to an Excel spreadsheet, as shown in Figure 4.20.

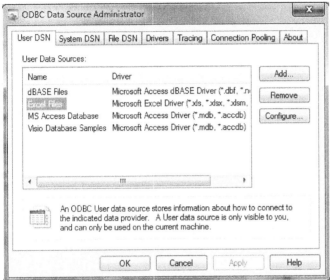

Figure 4.20 The ODBC Data Source Administrator.

The other way to get the ODBC Data Source Administrator open is from the control panel (**Control Panel** > **Administrative Tools** > **Data Sources (ODBC)**).

Click **Add**. On the Create New Data Source dialog box, select **Microsoft Excel Driver (*.xls, *.xlsx, *xlsb)** (Figure 4.21) and click **Finish**.

59

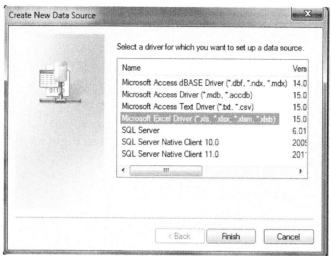

Figure 4.21 The Create New Data Source dialog box.

On the ODBC Microsoft Excel Setup dialog box, type **Sales** in the Data
Source Name. Choose **Excel 97-2000** as the Version, as shown in Figure
4.22.

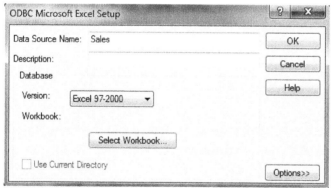

Figure 4.22 The ODBC Microsoft Excel Setup dialog box.

Click **Select Workbook** to launch yet another dialog box. In this one,
navigate to the **Sales.xls** file in
C:\Joes2Pros\SSRSCompanionFiles\Chapter4\Resources and click **OK** as
shown in Figure 4.23.

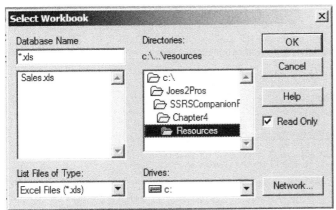

Figure 4.23 The Select Worbook dialog box.

Continue to click **OK** until all the dialog boxes are closed.

You now have an ODBC data source pointing to the Excel file that can be used by any program that works with ODBC.

The next step is to set up a data source inside SSDT pointing to the ODBC data source you just created. Go back to SSDT and your SSRS project. Right-click the **Shared Data Sources** found in the Solution Explorer and choose **Add new data source**. This opens up the Shared Data Source Properties dialog box, but you will configure it very differently this time than you did when the data was found in a SQL Server database.

In the **Name** field, type in **SalesExcel**. Click the **Type** list and take a look at the list of systems that SSRS can use as data sources (Figure 4.23).

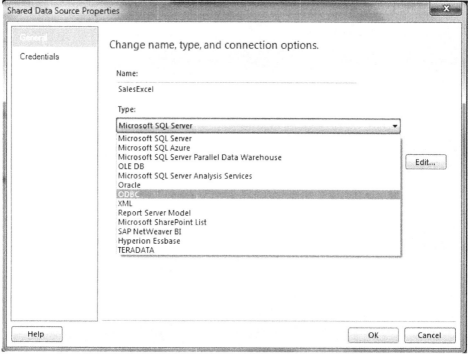

Figure 4.24 The Shared Data Source Properties dialog box.

Select **ODBC** and click **Edit**. This brings up the Connection Properties dialog box (Figure 4.24). In the **Use user or system data source name**, select **Sales**. This is the ODBC data source you set up earlier.

Figure 4.25 Connection Properties

Click **OK** twice. You should see the new Shared Data Source in the
Solution Explorer window (Figure 4.26).

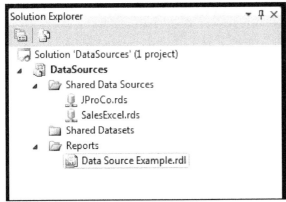

Figure 4.26 The Solution Explorer.

The next step is to create a new report. Right-click **Reports** and select **Add > New Item** (Figure 4.27).

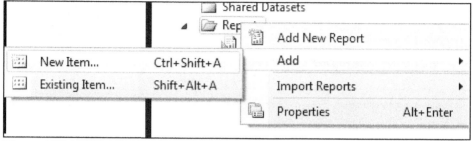

Figure 4.27 Add New Item.

When shown the list of items you can add, select **Report** and type **Excel** in the **Name**, and click **Add** (Figure 4.28).

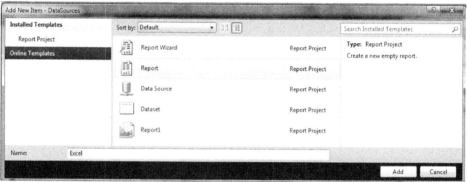

Figure 4.28 Choose Report (not Report Wizard).

The next step is to connect the data to the new report. On the left side, locate the **Report Data** window. If you don't see it, click **View > Report Data** from the toolbar. Right-click **Data Sources** and select **Add Data Source**.

On the **Data Source Properties** window, type **SalesExcel** in the **Name** field and **SalesExcel** under the **Use shared data source reference** text box. Figure 4.29 shows how the data source properties should look.

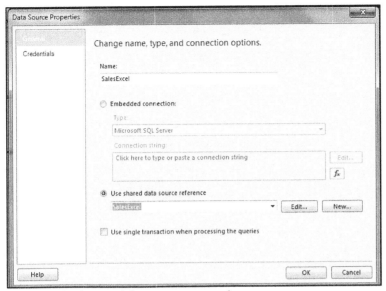

Figure 4.29 The Excel data source properties.

Click **OK**. Right-click **Datasets** and choose to **Add Dataset**. Type **Sales** in the **Name** field. Choose **Use a dataset embedded in my report**. Choose **SalesExcel** from the **Data source** list. Type the following query **SELECT * FROM [Sheet1$]**. Figure 4.30 shows how the dataset properties should look.

65

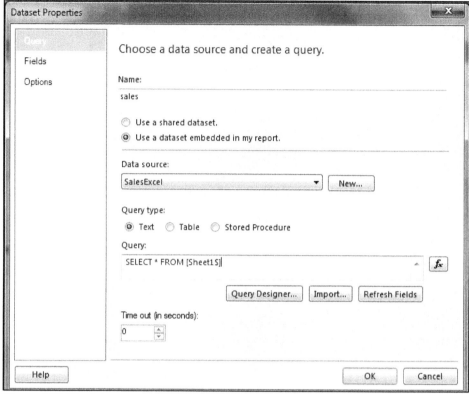

Figure 4.30 The dataset properties.

Click **OK**. You now have a data source pointing to the Excel file and a dataset that queries the spreadsheet (Figure 4.31).

66

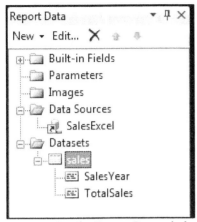

Figure 4.31 The Report Data window.

If you want to make sure you can actually create a report, go ahead and add a **Table** control to the report and add the fields to the cells.

You probably will not be creating reports from Excel spreadsheets in your job, but this excecise demonstrates that SSRS works with data that doesn't live in SQL Server.

Summary

Configuring the data source and dataset are critical for developing reports, but the best way to set these up can be confusing. This chapter walked you through setting up data sources and datasets and also recommended some best practices.

Be sure to use Shared Data Sources to save time when developing reports and managing them once they are deployed. There are certain exceptions, but most datasets will be embedded in the reports.

Points to Ponder – Connect to Your Data

1. A Data Source is a connection to your database.

2. You can connect to data from many sources, such as Oracle databases and Excel spreadsheets.

3. A shared data source can be reused in all the reports in your project.

4. To modify the properties of a data source, double click, don't right-click.

5. A dataset is the query, or request to the database for data.

6. You can use a query builder or write the query yourself.

7. You can create a dataset that is shared with other reports – that is great for parameter lists.

8. You can create a dataset that is embedded in the report – that is the most common method.

9. A dataset could also be a stored procedure.

Review Quiz – Chapter Four

1.) Why should you use a shared data source?

  O a. You can create just one shared data source for your entire company.
  O b. A shared data source can be used by all reports pointing to the same database.
  O c. Trick question! There is no such thing as a shared data source.
  O d. The only type of data source allowed in SSRS is a shared data source.

2.) How can you create a dataset?

  O a. With a stored procedure.
  O b. By typing the query in the query text box.
  O c. By using the Query Designer.
  O d. All of the above.

Answer Key

1) Only answer (b) is true. A shared data source points to one SQL Server and one database. Often multiple reports will pull data from the same database so they can use a shared data source. Using a shared data source is also helpful if something changes, for example, if the database is moved to a new server. Making one change will update multiple reports.

2) You have many choices when creating the dataset, including typing the query, using a stored procedure and designing the query with a query builder, so (d) is correct.

[NOTES]

70
www.Joes2Pros.com

Chapter 5.   SQL Server Data Tools

About 15 years ago, I agreed to spend an afternoon helping a neighbor learn how to use her computer. I was surprised to find out that the only program she knew how to use was Excel. Even if she wanted to type a letter and print it out, she did it in Excel. When working in IT, I often hear "when your only tool is a hammer everything looks like a nail." That was definitely the case with this person. She knew, well kind of knew, how to use Excel and didn't want to learn any other programs. Excel is a great tool, but not the best tool for everything.

Even though you could create a Reporting Services Report in a number of tools, including Notepad, the best tool for this job is SQL Server Data Tools (SSDT).

To make sure that you use design reports efficiently, you'll spend some time in this chapter learning more about SSDT so that you can be efficient when creating reports.

Projects and Solutions

Most people understand what Excel is and what you do to complete a project using Excel. While working within Excel, you will always work inside a workbook. A workbook is basically a container of spreadsheets and other components like graphs. You can create just one spreadsheet in Excel and work on that without ever needing a second spreadsheet in your workbook. If you need two spreadsheets, you can put both sheets in one workbook or one sheet in each workbook.

While working within SSDT, you will always work inside a project. A project is basically a container that allows you to organize your reports and the other components. You could create one project with dozens of reports and work with it for years without ever creating a second project or you could create a new project for every single report. My advice is to create separate projects for each subject matter. For example, in my previous job, I had a project for the reports I created for HR, a project for the Records department reports, and another project for the IT management reports. Having these three separate projects for this one company was a great solution. You can organize your reports any number of ways, so spend some time planning up front.

READER NOTE: If I wanted to have all three separate projects (HR, Records department and IT management) open at once in SSDT then that is possible and we will cover that next.

Within SSDT, it is possible to have multiple projects in a solution. Actually, even if you have one project it is still part of a solution. A solution can have multiple projects of the same type or projects of different types. If you have just one project in the solution, you may or may not see the solution depending on an SSDT setting. Figure 5.1 shows the Solution Explorer window with and without the Solution visible.

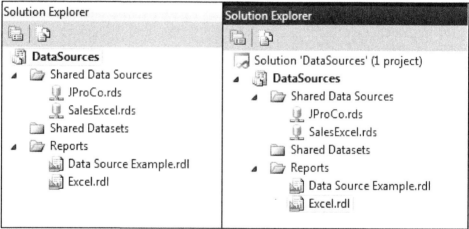

Figure 5.1 The Solution Explorer window.

To make the solution visible at all times, from the toolbar select **Tools > Options**. Select the **Projects and Solutions**, **General** tab. Check or uncheck **Always show solution** as you desire as shown in Figure 5.2.

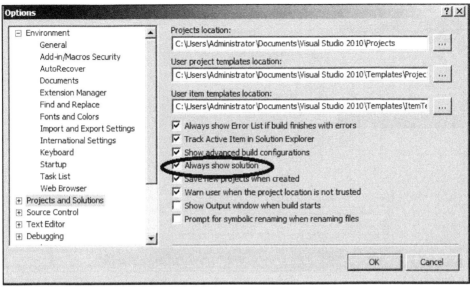

Figure 5.2 Always show solution.

Create a New Project

To create a new project, launch SSDT. From the toolbar, select **File > New > Project**. From there you will choose the appropriate project type. For this book, you will be creating Reporting Services Reports. Type in a name for your project, change the location to C:\Joes2Pros\SSRSCompanionFiles\Chapter5\Project and click **OK**. Figure 5.3 shows how the dialog box will look.

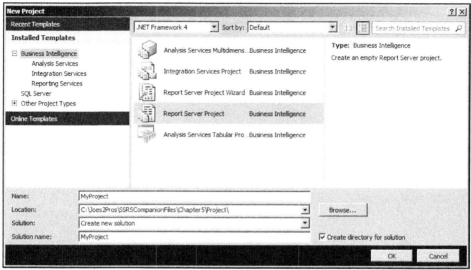

Figure 5.3 New Project.

Adding a project to an existing solution is very similar to just creating a new project. While you have a solution open in SSDT, from the File menu on the toolbar select **File** > **Add** >**New Project**. Another way to add a project is by right-clicking on the solution name and selecting **Add** > **New Project**. If your plan is to create reports, be sure to select **Report Server Project**.

Open an Existing Project

You will often need to get back to an existing report either to continue working where you left off or to add more reports to your project. Like many things in SSRS report development, there is more than one way to accomplish this task.

By default there is a page in Visual Studio called Start Page where you can see the list of the most recent projects you have worked on. Just click the project name, and it should open up. Figure 5.4 shows this page on my computer.

Figure 5.4 The Start Page.

The second method is useful especially if you have changed the settings so that the Start Page doesn't display when you open SSDT. From the File menu in the toolbar, you can open recently used projects from **File > Recent Project and Solutions**. Figure 5.5 shows how this looks.

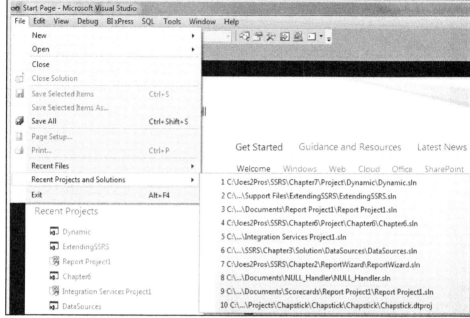

Figure 5.5 Open a new project from the File menu.

The last two methods are similar to working with any Windows program. You can navigate to the project solution files (sln) from **File > Open**. You can also navigate to the project solution file from the Windows Explorer and double-click it to open SSDT.

Toolbar Menus

The Visual Studio toolbar looks very similar to the toolbars found in other Microsoft products, at least before the new ribbon interface came out. Figure 5.6 shows the left side of the report toolbar.

Figure 5.6 The Visual Studio toolbar.

Many of the menus, and icons are found in other products, but a few are specific to SSRS. The lower left-hand side of the figure contains five icons just for SSRS. If you have SSDT open with a report in Design view, click each of these to find out what they do. These buttons will add a report header and footer, turn the grouping section on or off, and add rulers to the report.

The report menu also contains some SSRS specific options. Figure 5.7 shows the Report menu.

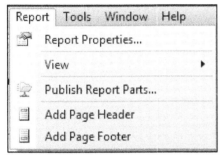

Figure 5.7 The Report menu.

If you followed along in Chapter 3, you have already modified some Text Box properties by bringing up the Textbox Property dialog box. You can also modify fonts and other Text Box properties by using the **Report Formatting** buttons. Figure 5.8 shows how that toolbar looks.

Figure 5.8 The Report Formatting menu.

If you don't see it, right-click on the toolbar and make sure to check **Report Formatting**.

SSDT Windows

You will work with four windows in SSDT while designing reports: **Solution Explorer**, **Properties**, **Report Data** and **Toolbox**. SSDT is part of Visual Studio. Visual Studio allows you to customize the environment so you can work the way you wish. Unfortunately, it is also possible to rearrange the windows until you can't find anything and it is difficult to work. Go ahead and experiment but remember that you can always select **Windows > Reset Windows Layout** from the toolbar to get everything back to the default.

Visual Studio has an Auto-Hide feature that allows you to hide and open a window by hovering the cursor over it. To turn on this feature click the push-pin icon at the right corner window (Figure 5.9).

Figure 5.9 The Auto-Hide push pin.

Once you enable the Auto-Hide feature, the window will collapse into the edge of the screen (Figure 5.10). To view the window just mouse over the window name to make it pop back out temporarily. This is a nice feature that gives you more room to work. To turn off Auto-Hide, just click the push-pin again when the window is open.

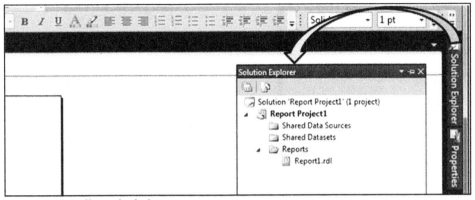

Figure 5.10 Collapsed windows.

Windows can also float instead of being attached to the side, and you can dock the windows in other places within the tool by dragging the windows around. Except for the Auto-Hide feature, I recommend that you leave the windows in the default locations.

If you have been following along with the examples so far, you probably have an idea about the purpose of each of the important windows, but next you'll learn even more.

Solution Explorer

The Solution Explorer is the place where you will find all the reports and project wide components you will use when building a report. It's the central location for all the work that you will do. Figure 5.9 shows the Solution Explorer with the project from Chapter 4 open.

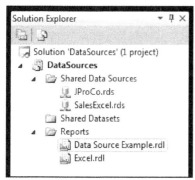

Figure 5.11 Solution Explorer.

The **Solution** folder will be visible if you have multiple projects or if you have enabled the **Always show solution** option found in **Tools > Options > Solutions and Projects**. Below the solution, you will see one or more projects. The project in Figure 5.11 is called **DataSources** from Chapter 4.

You will find several folders inside each project. The **Shared Data Sources** folder contains data sources. Each data source contains connection information which tells SSRS where to find the database used in the reports. To edit a data source, *do not* right-click and choose **Properties**. Be sure to double-click the data source. Data sources can also be embedded in reports, but the best practice is to create a shared data source that can be used by all the reports in your project. Review Chapter 4 to learn more about data sources.

The next folder is **Shared Datasets**. A dataset is the query, or command, that SSRS will send to the database server. The database server will respond with data that will be displayed on the report. Because queries are rarely shared among reports, you will usually not create shared data sets. There are some exceptions to this, such as parameter lists that will be used by more than one report. A parameter is an option when running the report such as the date or department. Often the report parameters will have lists of values so the user can select a valid value, and the list might apply to more than one report. Figure 5.12 shows a parameter with a parameter list.

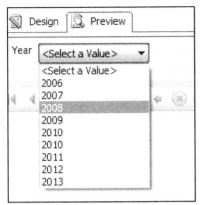

Figure 5.12 A parameter list.

A query for a parameter list is often set up as a shared dataset, but otherwise datasets should be embedded in the reports. See Chapter 4 to review creating datasets.

The **Reports** folder stores all the reports found in the project. To edit a report, double-click the report name. The report will then display in Design view in the middle of the work area. You can also add new reports to the project by right-clicking the folder and choosing **Add > New Item > Report**. You can start up the report wizard by right-clicking **Reports** and choosing **Add New Report**. You can also import an existing report from outside the project by right-clicking and selecting **Add > Existing Item**. You will then have to navigate to a report file with the RDL extension to bring it into the existing project.

If you accidently close the Solution Explorer, type **CTRL+ALT+L** or click **View > Solution Explorer** from the toolbar to get it back.

The Properties Window

If you followed along in Chapter 3, you found that much of the report development time is spent modifying the properties of text boxes. You can set many properties with special dialog boxes for the text box or other report objects that you are modifying. Most of the properties for the report objects can also be found in the **Properties** window. The **Properties** window is usually found on the right side of the screen. When the window is visible, you can see the context change as you click around on the report. Figure 5.13 shows how the **Properties** window looks when a text box is selected.

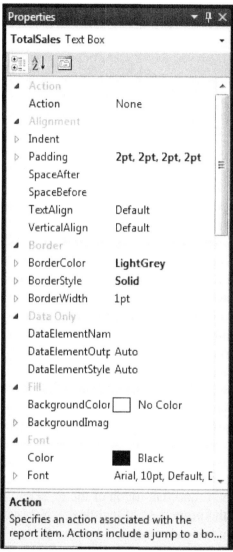

Figure 5.13 Properties for the TotalSales Text Box.

This view shows the properties organized by category. You can also click the **AZ** icon at the top to sort by property name.

In most cases, you will choose the property value from a dropdown list of possible values, but there are several other options you will learn about as you work through this book.

If you don't see the **Properties** window, hit **F4** to get it back.

The Report Data Window

Without data, there is no reason for reports. The **Report Data** window is where you manage the data sources, datasets, and parameters for individual reports. The **Report Data** window can be seen in Figure 5.14.

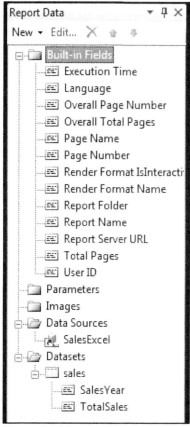

Figure 5.14 Report Data.

The **Built-in Fields** folder contains several useful information fields that you can drag directly onto your report. Generally, this information will be added to the header or footer of the report. Most commonly, reports will contain the number of pages and the execution time.

You will manage the report parameters in the **Parameters** folder. Figure 5.15 shows a typical **Parameter** dialog box.

84

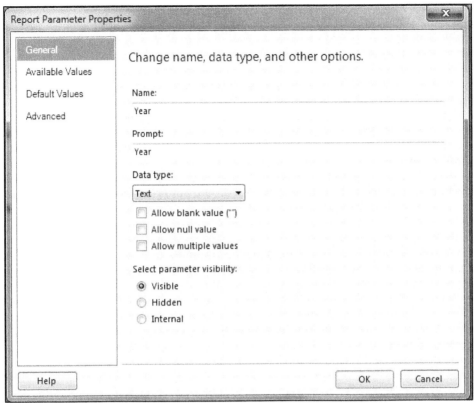

Figure 5.15 The Report Parameter Properties.

Properly configured report parameters make the report viewing experience more efficient and the report more user friendly. Within the **Parameters** dialog box, you can configure the parameter lists, default values, data types, and more. You will learn about report parameters in detail in Chapter 7.

Within the **Images** folder, you will store images that will be used in the report such as logos. To add an image, just right-click the folder and select **Add Image**. Navigate to an image file and select it.

The **Data Sources** folder stores data sources used in the report. Data sources contain the instructions for connecting to the database. Data sources can be embeded in the report or they may point to a project level shared data source. The data source in Figure 5.16 points to the shared data source from the Data Sources project from Chapter 4.

Figure 5.16 The JProCo data source.

While it is possible to create embedded data sources, the best practice is to create project-wide shared data sources to save time and effort.

Finally, at the bottom of the window, you will find the **Dataset** folder. Datasets are the queries, or database commands, that will be sent to the database server. The database server will return the data that satisfies the request. Datasets are usually created within this folder, embedding them into the reports. Most of the time report queries are unique to the report, but there are some situations where they are reused. In that case, shared datasets make sense.

The **Report Data** window is the heart of the report building environment. If you accidently close the window, you can get it back by typing **CTRL+ALT+D** or by selecting **View > Report Data** from the main menu.

The Toolbox

The Toolbox contains all of the building blocks you will use when developing reports. Figure 5.17 shows the contents of the Toolbox.

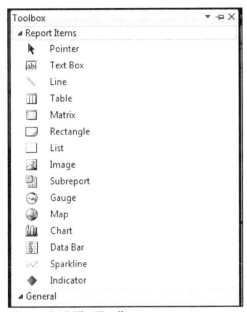

Figure 5.17 The Toolbox.

The Text Box and the Table are the most commonly used controls found in the Toolbox. To add a control, just select it and then click the **report design canvas**. Throughout this book, you will learn how to use these controls to create compelling reports for your organization. If you accidently close the Toolbox, you can get it back by typing **CTRL+ALT+X**.

Summary

You will be spending a lot of time working in SSDT, so it is important that you know how to work efficiently. There are four important windows: Solution Explorer, Properties, Report Data and Toolbox.

Points to Ponder – SQL Server Data Tools

1.   SSDT is the tool you will use to build SSRS reports.

2.   You will work in solutions that contain one or more projects.

3.   It is a best practice to create several projects to organize your work.

4.   A project can contain one or more reports and all the components that make up reports.

5.   The application menu looks like the menu found in many Windows programs.

6.   There are special menu items just for working with SSRS.

7.   You can format Text Boxes with the Report Formatting toolbar, the Properties window or the Text Box Properties dialog box.

8.   The Solution Explorer window contains the solution, projects, reports, project level data sources and project level datasets.

9.   The Properties window can be used to configure any report component or even the report itself.

10. The Report Data window is where you will manage the parameters, data sources and datasets specific to each report.

11. Built-in Fields, found in the Report Data, allow you to add common information like page count or execution time.

12. The Toolbox contains all the components to build a report.

13. To add a component to the report, just click the component and then click the report design canvas.

Review Quiz – Chapter Five

1.) Which statement is true?

O a) It is important to always embed data sources in the reports.
O b) Within SSDT, you work in projects with one or more solutions.
O c) Within SSDT, you cannot move windows around.
O d) Datasets are generally embedded in reports.

2.) What can't you find in the Report Data window? Select all that apply.

O a) Parameters
O b) Images
O c) Properties
O d) Datasets

3.) Where can you format a Text Box? Choose all that apply.

☐ a. The Toolbox.
☐ b. The Properties window.
☐ c. The Text Box Properties dialog.
☐ d. The Report Formatting menu.

Answer Key

1.) Answer (a) is not correct. It is better to create data sources at the project level.. Since you will work in solutions with one or more projects Answer (b) is not correct either. SSDT will allow you to move windows around any way you wish making C another incorrect answer. The correct answer is D. Since datasets are generally unique to the report, most datasets will be embedded in the report.

2.) All answers can be found except for A. You cannot format the Text Box with the Toolbox.

3.) The toolbox can only create new controls and does not change the formatting, so (a) is wrong. You cannot format the Text Box with the Toolbox. The Properties window, The Text Box Properties dialog, and the Report Formatting menu can call help to format a text box. This means (b), (c), and (d) are correct.

[NOTES]

Chapter 6.   Building a Report

Today's network and cable television is filled with reality shows. Since I love Karaoke, I enjoy watching "American Idol" and "The Voice". The roots of reality shows seen today go back decades to programs like "This Old House" and "The Gong Show". Years ago PBS featured cooking shows and shows with artists painting still lifes and scenery. The premise of the art programs was that you could follow along at home and create paintings just as good. I remember being impressed at the talent displayed as the artist created a beautiful work of art starting with a plain canvas, but I was not able to duplicate the works myself.

Designing a report is similar to creating a painting. In this chapter, you will start with a blank canvas and learn how to add and format the data to make an attractive report. The data is the most important part of the report, but if the report is not pleasing to the eye or is difficult to understand, the end users will not be happy.

Creating the Project and Report

In this chapter, you will create a report without the use of the Report Wizard. The steps in this section have already been covered in Chapters 4 and 5, but will be repeated here for your convenience. To learn more about any of these steps, refer to the previous chapters.

Launch SQL Server Data Tools. Click **New Project** and choose the **Report Server Project**. Type in a **Name** for your project, something like **Chapter6**, and save the project at C:\Joes2Pros\SSRSCompanionFiles\Chapter6\Project. Figure 6.1 shows how the screen should look. Click **OK**.

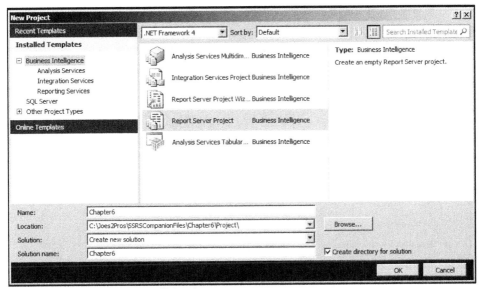

Figure 6.1 The New Project dialog box.

Once the project is created, add a new Shared Data Source. Right-click the **Shared Data Sources** folder and select **Add New Data Source**. Name the data source **JProCo**. Click **Edit** to configure the connection properties. Fill in the **Server name**, which will probably be **Localhost** or **Localhost\SQLExpress**. Select the **JProCo** database. Figure 6.2 shows how the Connection Properties dialog box should look.

Figure 6.2 The Connection Properties.

Click **OK** to accept the Connection Properties and **OK** again to accept the Shared Data Source Properties.

Create a new report by right-clicking the **Reports** folder and choosing **Add > New Item**. Select the **Report** item and type a report name. The report name can include spaces and will actually be what the end user will see when running the report. Name the report **Employee Sales**. Figure 6.3 shows how the Add New Item dialog box might look.

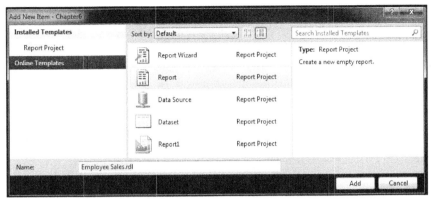

Figure 6.3 Add New Item dialog box.

Click **Add**. Now you should see the data source and the report in the Solution Explorer, as shown in Figure 6.4.

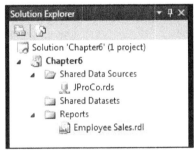

Figure 6.4 The new report in the Solution Explorer.

Double-click the report to open it in Design view. The next step is to create a data source for the report. In the **Report Data** window right-click **Data Sources** and select **Add Data Source**. Name the new data source **JProCo** and select **Use shared data source reference**. Select the **JProCo** data source from the dropdown list. The data source should look like Figure 6.5.

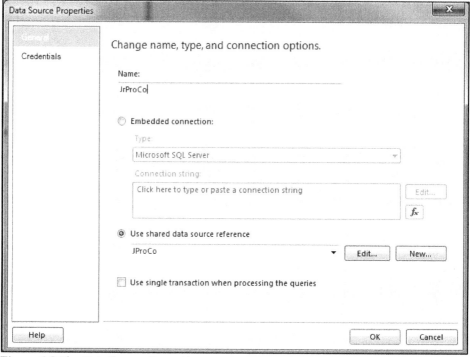

Figure 6.5 The Data Source Properties.

Click **OK**. The next step is to create a dataset. Right-click the **Dataset** folder in the **Report Data** window and choose **Add Dataset**. Name the dataset **EmployeeSales**. Select **Use a dataset embedded in my report** and select the **JProCo** data source. Click **Import** and open the **Sales by Employee.sql** file found at C:\Joes2Pros\SSRSCompanionFiles\Chapter6\Resources. The Dataset Properties dialog box should look like Figure 6.6.

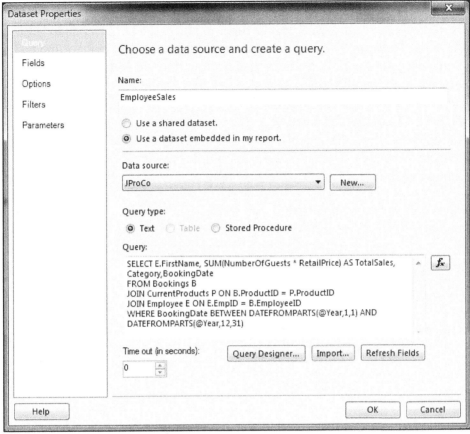

Figure 6.6 The Dataset Properties.

Click **OK**. Now, with all the prerequisites in place, you are ready to build your report!

Adding a Table

The Table control is a grid that displays data from a dataset similar to a spreadsheet. It is the most common way to display data in Reporting Services, and you will learn how to display data in other controls later in the book.

97

Begin by selecting the Table control from the Toolbox and dragging it to the report design canvas. With the table in place, the next step is to fill in the cells. There are two ways to add the fields to the data cells of the table. You can select the field from the dataset found in the **Report Data** window and drag it to the data cell. The other method is to hover the cursor over the right side of the cell. When you do, a list of possible fields appears. Clicking a field adds it to the cell. Another helpful feature is that the field name is automatically added to the header cells. You can edit the headers as needed. To add additional columns to the table right-click a column and choose **Insert Column > Right**.

Fill out the grid, as shown in Figure 6.7.

	Booking Date	Category	First Name	Total Sale
≡	[BookingDate]	[Category]	[FirstName]	[TotalSale]

Figure 6.7 The table with fields filled in.

You can now preview the report by clicking **Preview**. When prompted, type in **2006** as the year. Click **View Report**. Figure 6.8 shows the report so far.

Employee Sales.rdl [Design] ✕

🖉 Design   📄 Preview

Year 2006

◀◀ ◀ 1   of 2 ? ▶ ▶◀ | ⬅ ⊗ ⟳ | 🖶 🗐 📖 ⬇ ▾ | 100%   ▾

Booking Date	Category	First Name	Total Sale
7/12/2006 12:00:00 AM	Medium-Stay	James	3429.0880
12/5/2006 12:00:00 AM	No-Stay	Barbara	1012.8170
5/15/2006 12:00:00 AM	Medium-Stay	Terry	632.1720
8/3/2006 12:00:00 AM	LongTerm-Stay	Sally	1580.4300
6/13/2006 12:00:00 AM	Overnight-Stay	Eric	672.8832
1/24/2006 12:00:00 AM	No-Stay	Sally	652.0200

Figure 6.8 The report preview.

Formatting the Report

At this point you can see the data, but the report looks a bit bland, not attractive at all. Formatting columns, rows or just individual cells is easy. The easiest way is to use the **Report Formatting** menu which is similar to formatting in other Windows programs. Figure 6.9 shows the menu. If you don't see the **Report Formatting** menu on your screen, right-click the toolbar area and select **Report Formatting**.

Figure 6.9 The Report Formatting menu.

To get started, switch back to Design view. Select the row containing the column headings and click the bold icon, which looks like a B. Next, click the background color icon which looks like a pen. Choose **Blue** and click **OK**. Since Blue is a dark color, change the foreground color to white, by clicking the foreground color icon which looks like an A.

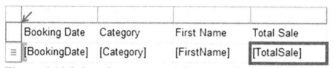

| Booking Date | Category | First Name | Total Sale |
| [BookingDate] | [Category] | [FirstName] | [TotalSale] |

Figure 6.10 Select the row containing the column headings.

Format the BookingDate cell by right-clicking and choosing **Text Box Properties**. Choose the **Number** page. Select the **Date** category and choose the **1/31/2000** format. The properties should look like Figure 6.11.

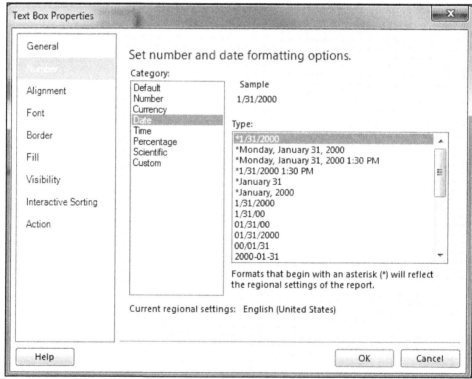

Figure 6.11 Format the date.

100

Click **OK**. Format the **[TotalSale]** cell as **Currency** with no decimal places and a 1000 separator. Figure 6.12 shows how you should configure the **[TotalSale]** properties.

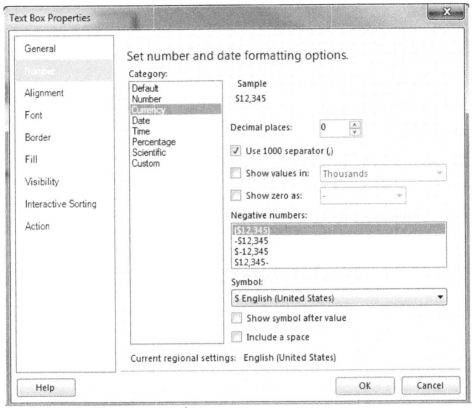

Figure 6.12 The Text Box Properties.

Click **OK** to accept. Numbers generally look better if they are aligned on the right. Select the **Total Sale** column and then click the **Align Right** icon in the toolbar. Right align the Booking Date column as well.

The next thing to consider is sorting. You can sort the data by any of the fields in the table. To set up sorting, right-click a row or column handle and choose **Tablix Properties** (Figure 6.13).

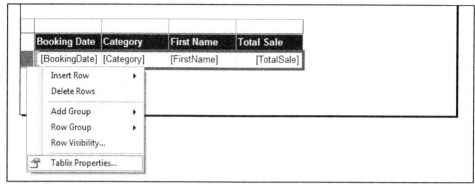

Figure 6.13 The column handle.

*READER NOTE: **Tablix** is the combination of the words table and matrix, the two grid types used to display data.*

In the **Tablix Properties** dialog box, select **Sorting**. Click **Add** and choose the **BookingDate** field. The dialog box should look like Figure 6.14.

Figure 6.14 The table or "Tablix" properties.

Click **OK** to accept the change. Preview the report to see how the report looks. It should look something like Figure 6.15.

Booking Date	Category	First Name	Total Sale
1/7/2006	LongTerm-Stay	Lee	$5,412
1/13/2006	LongTerm-Stay	Eric	$6,752
1/15/2006	LongTerm-Stay	Lee	$11,820
1/15/2006	Overnight-Stay	Lisa	$258
1/17/2006	LongTerm-Stay	Sally	$3,189
1/20/2006	Overnight-Stay	Terry	$567
1/24/2006	No-Stay	Sally	$652
1/25/2006	Overnight-Stay	Barbara	$2,519
2/5/2006	Medium-Stay	Lee	$7,218
2/7/2006	LongTerm-Stay	Eric	$6,231
2/9/2006	LongTerm-Stay	Eric	$3,640
2/12/2006	No-Stay	Lee	$726

Figure 6.15 The report with formatting.

Page Headers and Footers

So far your simple report looks pretty good, but is lacking several things such as a title and page numbers. These items work best in the report header and footer. To add a header to the report, switch back to Design view and click the **Add Header** icon in the menu. See Figure 6.16 to see the icon.

Figure 6.16 The Add Header icon.

Add a report footer by clicking the **Report Footer** icon which is next to the **Report Header** icon. Click a column in the table and then click the square in the intersection of the column and row handles. Figure 6.17 shows the area to click.

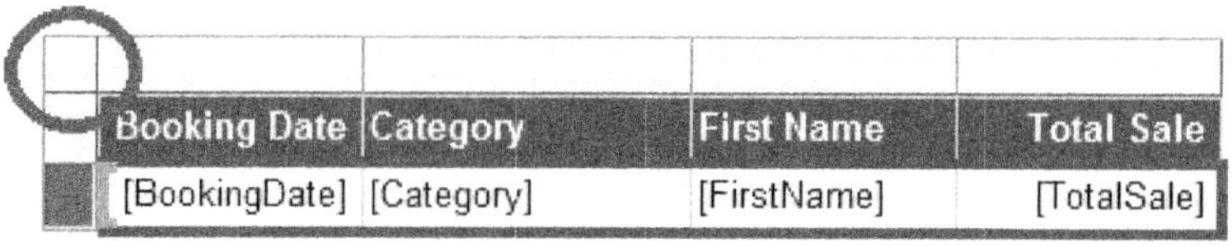

Figure 6.17 The column and row handle intersection.

When you click the square, the column and row handles disappear, and you will see a small icon with four arrows, as shown in Figure 6.18.

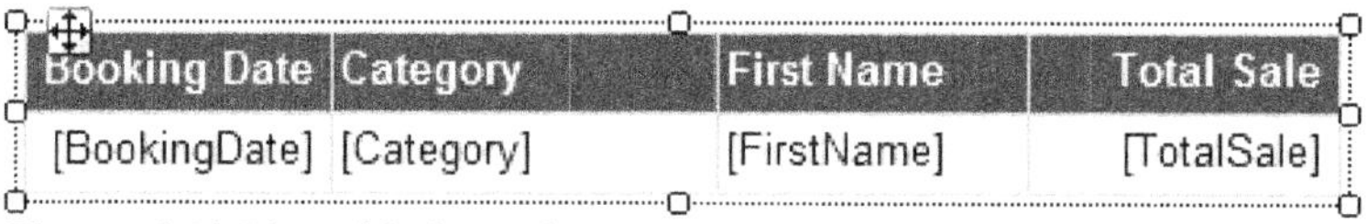

Figure 6.18 The table is ready to move.

Click the arrow icon and drag the table to the left and right underneath the header. Find the line separating the body of the report from the footer. Hover the cursor over the line until the cursor turns into a double arrow. Click and drag the line up to the table. Figure 6.19 shows how the report design should look.

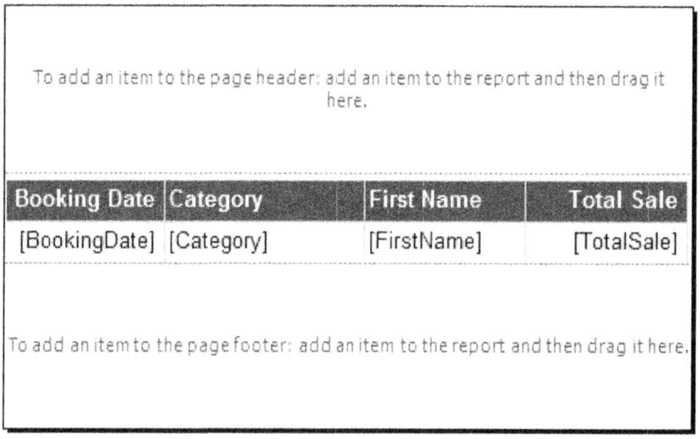

Figure 6.19 The report design with header and footer in place.

Add a Text Box to the left edge of the header. Hover over the right side of the Text Box until the cursor tuns to a double arrow. Drag the right edge over to the right until it lines up with the right edge of the table. Click into the texbox and type **Employee Sales**. Increase the size of the font to 16pt by clicking the edge of the Text Box and then changing the font size in the design menu. Center the text of the Text Box by clicking the **Center** icon, as shown in Figure 6.20.

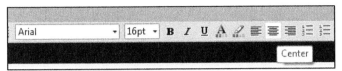

Figure 6.20 The Center icon.

Remove some of the extra space in the header by dragging up the line between the body of the report and the heading.

Report users appreciate the extra touches you can add to the report like page numbers. SSRS makes adding these little details easy. From the Report Data window, expand the **Built-in Fields** folder and drag **Page Number** to the footer. Drag **Execution Time** to the footer. Rearrange these Text Boxes so that they line up. You can use the blue lines that show up when moving Text Boxes around to help as shown in Figure 6.21.

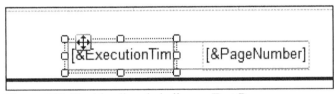

Figure 6.21 The blue lines help line up Text Boxes.

READER NOTE: *You may have noticed that there are two page number fields, Page Number and Overall Page Number. For a simple report, it doesn't matter which one you use. For more complex reports using groups, the Page Number field starts over for each group while the Overall Page Number gives the actual page for the entire report.*

Preview the report and note anything that needs to be adjusted. Be sure to scroll down to the bottom of the report to take a look at the footer. Figure 6.22 shows the footer.

Figure 6.22 The footer.

At a minimum, you should expand the Execution Time Text Box. Alternatively, you can reformat the Text Box to display just the date without the time. Use the skills you have learned in this chapter to modify the date format of the Execution Time texbox.

The Page number Text Box can be modified to show more information. Make sure the report is in Design view. Right-click the Text Box and choose **Expression** to bring up the Expression dialog box. SSRS allows you to base most of the properties of a Text Box on an expression. Expressions are similar to formulas in Excel.

You will see a formula in the Expression dialog box **=Globals!PageNumber**. Change that formula to **="Page " & Globals!PageNumber & " of " & Globals!TotalPages & " pages"**, as shown in Figure 6.23.

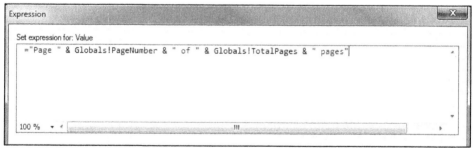

Figure 6.23 The Total Pages expression.

Click **OK**. Now the Text Box will display **<<Expr>>** which means the value is based on an expression. Expand the width of the Text Box to about double the original size. Now preview the report to see how the footer looks, as shown in Figure 6.24.

```
4/25/2013     Page 1 of 3 pages
```

Figure 6.24 The new formatted footer.

If you scroll to the second or third page of the report, you will notice that the table headings only show up on page 1. Click back to Design view to fix this issue. In the very bottom of the report you will find the Grouping section. Right now you don't have to worry about the section until Chapter 8 except to fix this small issue. On the right side of the section you will find a small arrow. Click the arrow and select **Advanced Mode**. This displays several areas labeled **(Static)**. Select the **(Static)** area in the **Row Groups** area, as shown in Figure 6.25.

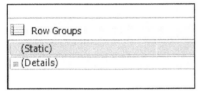

Figure 6.25 The static area.

While **(Static)** is selected, hit F4 to open the Properties window. Find the **RepeatOnNewPage** property and change it to **True** (Figure 6.26).

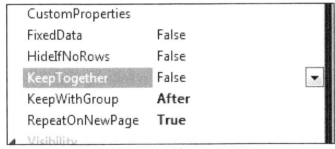

Figure 6.26 Keep with group setting.

Now preview the report again to see that the column headers are repeated on each page.

Print Settings

In my previous job as a database administrator for a large law firm, I created many reports. One complaint I often received when I first began working with SSRS was that the report looked great on the screen but printed alternating blank pages or each page was printed across two pages. In this section, you will learn how to avoid this issue so that reports print properly every time.

By default, a report will print properly, but as you work building the report, you may accidently increase the report width or maybe the data needs more than 8 ½ inches across to display. To simulate this issue, make sure the rulers are showing while in Design view. To turn the rulers on, click the Ruler icon in the toolbar. Drag the right edge of the report so that it is at least seven inches wide.

Now preview the report and click the **Print Layout** icon (Figure 6.27) to see how the report will look printed. This button allows you to toggle between print view and the regular preview mode. Page through the report in print preview mode to see that the report will have alternating pages with just the header and footer showing.

Figure 6.27 The Print Layout icon.

The icon to the right of the **Print Layout** icon allows you to change the report from portrait to landscape and change the margins. These settings are important, but may not help if the report itself is too wide. Switch back to Design view. The width of the printed report equals the width shown on the ruler plus the left margin plus the right margin. For example, if the report is seven inches wide and the margins are each one inch, the report is not going to fit on 8.5 X 11 inch paper in portrait mode.

To fix this, be sure that the report is not wider than it needs to be by dragging the right side in. To adjust the report margins, from the toolbar, choose **Report > Report Properties**. Figure 6.28 shows all the options.

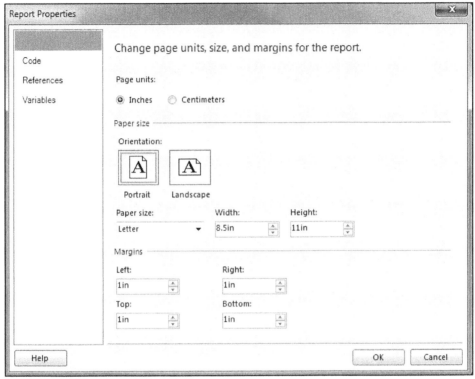

Figure 6.28 The report options.

Within this dialog box, you can change the orientation, paper size and adjust the margins. Make sure that the width of the report plus the right and left margins do not exceed the width of the paper. Click **OK** to save the settings and preview the report again in **Print Layout** mode to make sure that the report will print properly.

If you get in the habit of always viewing the report in the Print Layout mode, you will avoid a large number of complaints from your end users.

Summary

In this chapter you learned how to create a simple report without using a wizard. Just displaying the data will not be enough. You must spend some time formatting the data as well as adding useful header and footers. Take a look at the report in Print Layout to make sure that printing the report will not waste paper by printing blank pages.

Points to Ponder – Building a Report

1. To add data from a dataset to the report, pull a Table control to the report canvas from the Toolbox.

2. Add the fields to the table by dragging fields from the dataset to the table or hover over the cell in the table and choose the field from the icon.

3. You can modify the format, font, color and size of cells by right-clicking and choosing Properties or use the Properties window.

4. The width of columns can be changed by dragging the borders.

5. Right-click and select **Insert Column** > **Right** to add more fields to the report.

6. You can add a page header for any text you want to show up at the top of every page like a Title from the Report item in the menu.

7. Add a page footer for text you want to show up at the bottom of every page like Page Number from the Report item in the menu.

8. Adjust the report width and modify the margins to avoid printing blank pages in the report.

9. In the Report properties, you can change the paper size and orientation.

Review Quiz – Chapter Six

1.)   Which statement is true?

O a)   Once you drag a table to the report, you cannot move it to a different location on the report canvas.

O b)   Reports will always print perfectly without modifying the margins or report width.

O c)   When dragging items around on the canvas, blue lines will help you align the objects.

O d)   It is not possible in SSRS to base Text Box values on expressions.

2.)   Where are the Page Number and Execution Time fields located?

O a)   In the Toolbox window.

O b)   In the Report Data window.

O c)   In the toolbar menu.

O d)   In the Solution Explorer window.

3)   What is a Matrix report?

O a)   A type of chart.

O b)   A report where some of the data is pivoted as column headers.

O c)   A report that is made up of two or more sections.

O d)   A report where the data is displayed from right to left.

Answer Key

1.)   Answer (a) is not correct. You can move the Table control around on the canvas. Answer (b) is not correct either. It is easy to create a report that prints alternating blank pages. Be sure to check the print layout and adjust the report properties as needed. Answer (d) is not correct. You can base Text Box values and other properties on expressions. You will learn more about expressions in Chapter 7. When you move the objects around the canvas, blue lines appear to help you align the objects, so answer (c) is the correct answer.

2.)   The Page Number and Execution Time fields can be found in the Report Data window, Built-in Fields folder, making (b) the correct answer.

3)   A matrix report pivots one or more fields as column headers. For example, the sample report in this chapter pivots the employee name field as a column. This makes (b) the correct answer.

[NOTES]

Chapter 7.   Make Your Report Dynamic

Imagine that you have just received a request for a report with very precise specifications. The report should display the total sales for last year by category and month. You quickly create the report, check to make sure it prints correctly, and send the link to your supervisor. Within a couple of days, you get another request for the same report, but it should display the sales for this year. Oh, and by the way, can you include the ability to change the sort order by month, category or total? And it would really be great if it was possible to click any line and see the details.

In my career as a database administrator, I often created reports for some of the departments in the firm, and scenarios like this were all too common. I quickly learned to ask questions and anticipate what the requester might ask for next. I rarely created a report without providing options such as parameters.

In this chapter, you will learn how to make reports dynamic. It will save you time and make you look like an SSRS rock star!

Create the Reports

You will work with two reports in this chapter: a summary report and a detail report. In order to give you some more practice with the basics, you will create the reports.

To get started open SSDT and create a new project. The project should be created in the C:\Joes2Pros\SSRSCompanionFiles\Chapter7\Project folder and named **Dynamic**. Figure 7.1 shows how the dialog box should look.

Figure 7.1 The New Project dialog box.

Add a new shared data source pointing to your local SQL Server, named **JProCo** that points to the **JProCo** database on the LocalHost. See Chapter 4 if you need help setting it up. Figure 7.2 shows what the connection properties will look like if you have a default instance of SQL Server.

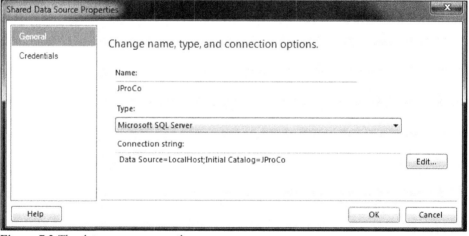

Figure 7.2 The data source properties.

Add a new report by right-clicking the **Report** folder and choosing **Add > New Item**. Select **Report** and name the report **Sales Summary**. Figure 7.3 shows how the **Add New Item** dialog box should look.

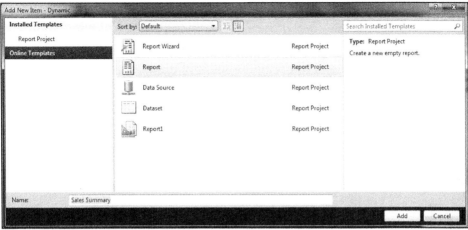

Figure 7.3 Add new item.

Click **Add**. If the new report does not open in Design mode, double-click it in the Solution Explorer to open it. The next step is to set up the data source in the **Report Data** window. If you don't see the window, type **CTRL + ALT + D**. Right-click on **Data Sources** and choose **Add New Data Source**. You will create a data sorce that points to the project's shared data source. The Data Source Properties dialog box should look like Figure 7.4.

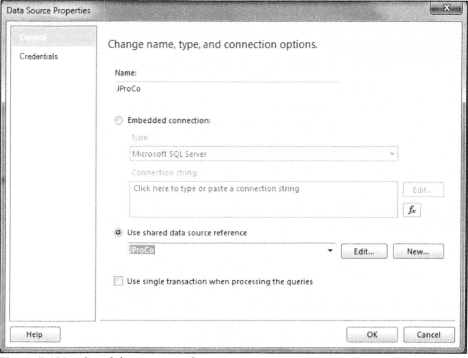

Figure 7.4 Use shared data source reference.

Click **OK**. Now create a new dataset that is embedded in the report by right-clicking the **Datasets** folder in the **Report Data** window and selecting **Add New Dataset**. You will use the query that can be found in the SalesSummary.sql file found in the C:\Joes2Pro\SSRS\Chapter7\Resources folder. After configuring the properties, the dataset should look like Figure 7.5.

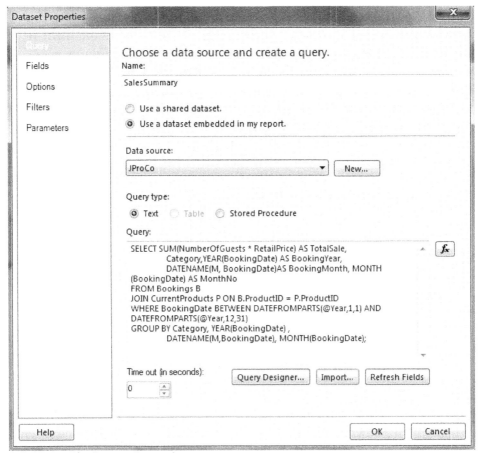

Figure 7.5 The Dataset Properties.

Be sure to import the query; don't try to type it in from the figure. Click **OK**. The next step is to add a table to the design canvas. From the Toolbox, drag a Table control to the report. If you don't see the Toolbox, type **CTRL + ALT + X**. Configure the fields in the table as shown in Figure 7.6. To add fields, drag them from the Report Data window.

Category	Booking Month	Total Sale
[Category]	[BookingMonth]	[TotalSale]

Figure 7.6 The table fields.

Format the report, adding a header with a title, a footer with the page number and an execution date. These fields can be found in the **Built-in Fields** folder in **Report Data**. To turn on the **Header** and **Footer** areas, choose **Report > Add Page Header** and **Report > Add Page Footer**. Format the cells by using the **Report Formatting** menu icons in the toolbar. Also be sure to format the [TotalSale] field as currency. See Chapters 3 and 6 for more information on these tasks.

Once you are done, the report design should look something like Figure 7.7.

Figure 7.7 The report design.

When you preview the report, you are prompted for a year. Enter the year **2006** and click **View Report**. It should look something like Figure 7.8.

Sales Summary

Category	Booking Month	Total Sale
LongTerm-Stay	April	$14,723
LongTerm-Stay	August	$5,069
LongTerm-Stay	December	$8,871
LongTerm-Stay	February	$9,870
LongTerm-Stay	January	$27,173
LongTerm-Stay	July	$7,352
LongTerm-Stay	June	$4,265
LongTerm-Stay	March	$13,210
LongTerm-Stay	May	$6,016
LongTerm-Stay	November	$24,108
LongTerm-Stay	October	$29,307

Figure 7.8 The formatted report.

Instead of giving you all the steps to create the details report, see if you can figure it out. Be sure to look up anything that you are not sure about.

You should create the report with the following specifications:

- The new report should be called Sales Details (Sales Details.rdl).
- The data source for this report should be called JProCo and be based on the JProCo shared data source.
- The dataset should be called SalesDetails and should be based on the query from the SQL script at this location - C:\Joes2Pros\SSRSCompanionFiles\Chapter7\Resources\SalesDetails.sql.
- The body of the report should be a 3 column table to hold BookingDate, Category, and TotalSale fields.
- The header should display "Sales Details" in a big font.

- The footer should hold two text boxes for the report Execution Time and the Overall Page Number.
- The BookingDate should be formatted as a month/day/year.
- The TotalSale field should be formatted as Currency with no decimals and having the 1000 separator (,).

The **Sales Details** report should look like Figure 7.9 in Design view when you are done.

Figure 7.9 The Sales Details report.

When you preview the report, type in **2006** for the year, **10** for the month and **LongTerm-Stay** for the category. Figure 7.10 shows how the report will look.

Sales Details

Booking Date	Category	Total Sale
10/11/2006	LongTerm-Stay	$3871
10/11/2006	LongTerm-Stay	$4914
10/28/2006	LongTerm-Stay	$10818
10/1/2006	LongTerm-Stay	$3401
10/20/2006	LongTerm-Stay	$6304

5/29/2013   1

Figure 7.10 The Sales Details report preview.

Parameters

The most common way to give control to the users of your reports is to provide parameters. So far, if you have been following along with the book, you have seen the Year parameter used on all the reports. To preview the reports, you had to enter a year, such as 2006. Allowing the end user to type a value in a text box is the most basic use of parameters, but there is so much more you can do.

In this section, you will learn about some of the other features.

Configuring Parameters

You may be wondering how the report automatically knew to create the Year parameter. Double-click the Sales Summary report to open it in Design view. If you take a close look at the Query property of the SalesSummary dataset, you'll see the @Year parameter as part of the SQL command as shown in Figure 7.11.

123

```
SELECT SUM(NumberOfGuests * RetailPrice) AS TotalSale,
        Category,YEAR(BookingDate) AS BookingYear,
        DATENAME(M, BookingDate)AS BookingMonth, MONTH
(BookingDate) AS MonthNo
FROM Bookings B
JOIN CurrentProducts P ON B.ProductID = P.ProductID
WHERE BookingDate BETWEEN DATEFROMPARTS(@Year,1,1) AND
DATEFROMPART(@Year,1,31)
GROUP BY Category, YEAR(BookingDate) ,
        DATENAME(M,BookingDate), MONTH(BookingDate);
```

Figure 7.11 The parameters in the query.

Whenever your query contains an expression in the WHERE clause starting with @, SSRS turns it into a parameter. If your report is based on a stored procedure with parameters, report parameters will also be automatically created.

When the parameter is created in this way, it has the default properties which are very simple. This allows the end user to type in any value, even a value of the wrong data type. Open the **Parameters** folder found in the Report Data window. Double-click the **@Year** parameter to view the properties. Figure 7.12 shows how the properties on the **General** page will look.

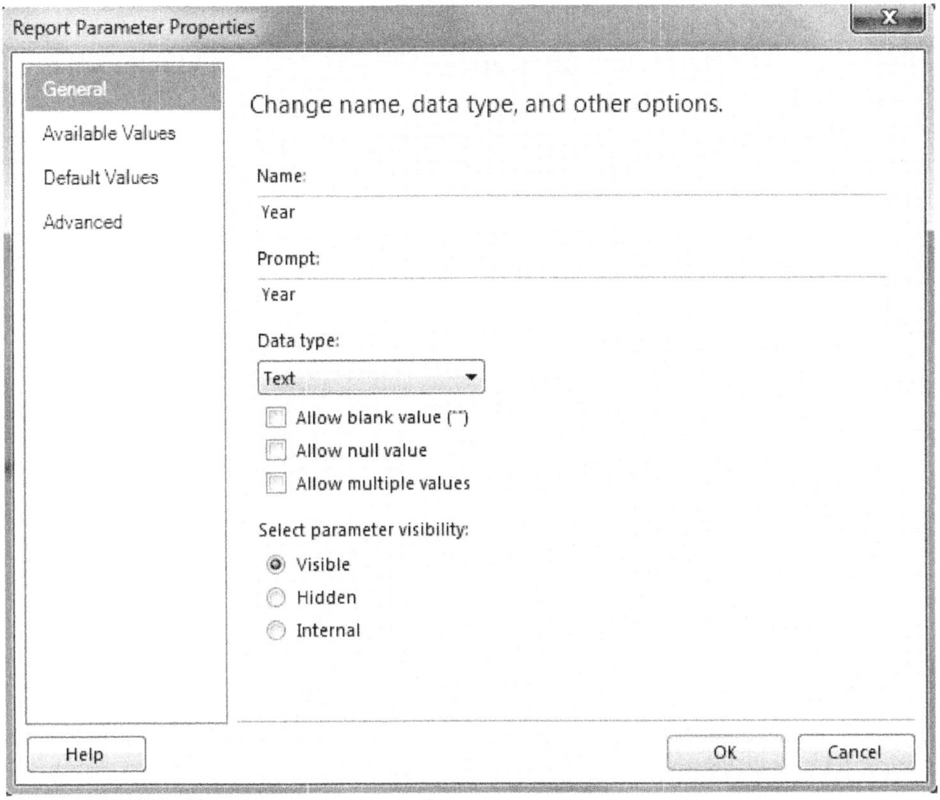

Figure 7.12 The Year parameter properties.

Instead of allowing the end user to type in any value, you can restrict the list of values based on a hard-coded list or a dataset. First, you will learn how to create the hard-coded list. Click **Available Values** and choose **Specify Values**. Click **Add**. You'll see an area appear where you can type a **Label** and a **Value**. The label is what the end user will see. The value is the value that the query needs. For example, imagine a Department table with a DeptID value needed for the query and a DeptDescription for the human who will run the report and hasn't memorized all the DeptID values. The DeptDescription would be the label and the DeptID would be the value. A value of 2006 for the @Year parameter makes a good label as well.

In this case both Label and Value are the same. In **Label** and **Value**, type **2006**. Click **Add** again, and fill in **2007**. The properties should look like Figure 7.13.

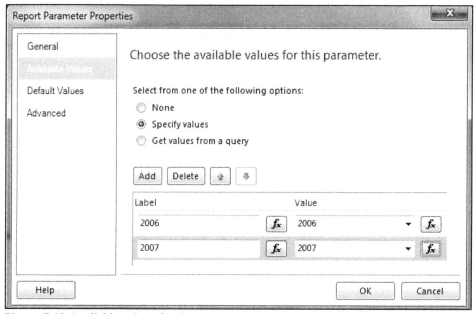

Figure 7.13 Available values for the parameters.

Click **OK**. Now preview the report. Instead of typing in a year, you will choose the value from the dropdown list as shown in Figure 7.14.

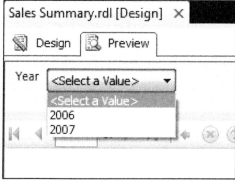

Figure 7.14 Available values for a parameter.

126

You could go back and manually enter several more years. But new year values will keep getting added as time goes on. To make sure that the choices are always valid, it is best to base the parameter on a query so that it is dynamic. Go back to Design view and create a new dataset and name it **Year**. Import the query found at C:\Joes2Pros\SSRSCompanionFiles\Chapter7\Resources\YearParameter.sql. The Dataset should look like Figure 7.15.

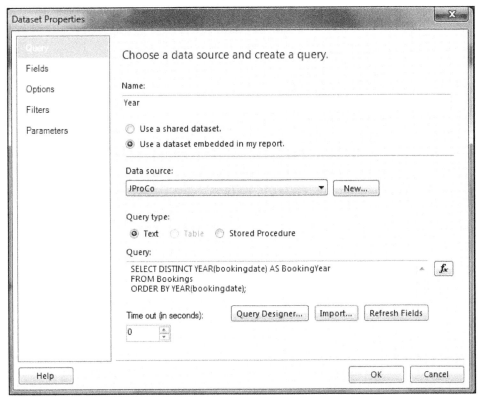

Figure 7.15 The dataset properties for the parameter list.

Click **OK**. Now double-click the **Year** parameter and click **Available Values**. Choose **Get values from a query**. Select **Year** for the **Dataset** property, and **BookingYear** for both the **Label** and **Value**. Click **OK** and preview the report. You should now see the list of possible years based on the actual data as shown in Figure 7.16.

Figure 7.16 The dynamically created parameter list.

Default Parameters

If there is a value that the end user will almost always choose, you can define that upfront so that it does not have to be entered at all. Open up the **Year** parameter and click **Default Values**. Select **Specify Values** and click **Add**. Type **2006** as the **Value**. In this case, the only property that must be filled in is the value that the query needs. The dialog box should look like Figure 7.17.

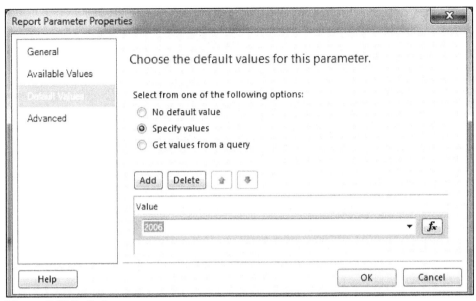

Figure 7.17 Default parameters.

Click **OK** and preview the report. Instead of waiting for you to select or type in a value, the report will automatically run. If you wish to select a different value, go ahead and choose it and then click **Run Report**.

Date and True/False Parameters

Most of the time a parameter and the data type of a parameter will be text or a number. The end user will either type in a value or select a value from a list you provide. You can also create parameters that allow the end user to select the date from a calendar control, called a date-picker. The other type of selection for the end user is to click either true or false instead of pulling the values from a list. Figure 7.18 shows an example of using these two types of parameters.

READER NOTE: The examples in the Date and True/False Parameters section are not part of a report built-in this chapter.

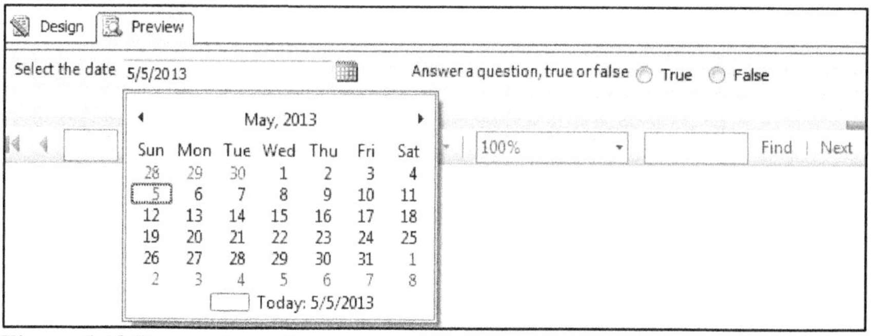

Figure 7.18 Date and true/false parameters.

This next step should not be done in your report and you do not have a parameter called **TheDate**. If you were to change this parameter type from the default text, modify the Data Type property found on the **General** page of the parameter (Figure 7.19).

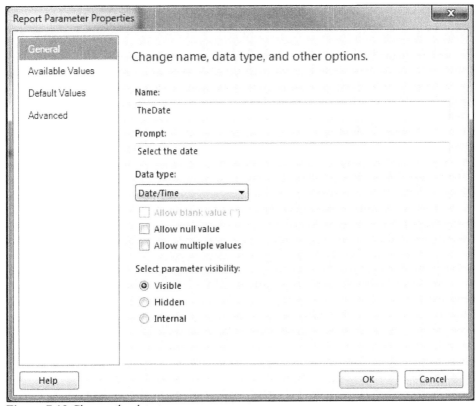

Figure 7.19 Change the data type.

You can also force the end user to type in whole numbers for a particular parameter value.

Display the Parameter Value on the Report

Imagine that you have delivered the new report with the ability to change the year by the use of parameters. Now when the report is printed, you can see the data and the date that it was printed, but you can't see which year was chosen to filter the data. The next enhancement is to provide the parameter value right on the report so that the report is actually meaningful.

Make sure you have the **Sales Summary** report open in Design view. Make sure there is some room in the report header underneath the title. If not, just drag the title up higher and you may have to make the header a bit taller. From the **Built-in Fields** folder in the **Report Data** window, drag the **@Year** parameter to the header as shown in Figure 7.20.

Figure 7.20 The Year parameter.

If you preview the report, you will now see the year you typed in under the title. To make this even better, you will add the parameter to the title itself. Go back to design view and delete the year Text Box. Right-click on the Sales Summary title Text Box and select Expressions. Change the formula to **="Sales Summary for " & Parameters!Year.Value** as shown in Figure 7.21.

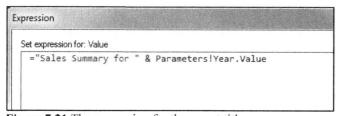

Figure 7.21 The expression for the report title.

Now when you preview the report it will display the year chosen in the report title as shown in Figure 7.22.

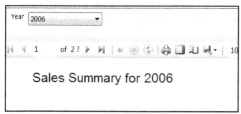

Figure 7.22 New report title.

Sorting

One of the most interesting complaints that I have ever heard about a report I created was that the end user was not able to sort the report properly when she exported it to Excel! After working with her to make sure I understood all the requirements and asking for feedback, she did not express how she wanted to see the data sorted. I had assumed that the way I chose to sort the data was the way she wanted to see the data. To get around this issue, she was exporting the report to Excel instead of asking me to make a simple change. In fact, I found out that she always exported SSRS reports to Excel.

You can configure the table sort by a particular column or columns, but you can also allow the end user to sort the report on the fly. To get started with sorting, make sure you are working with the Sales Summary report in Design view. Right-click a column of the table and choose **Tablix Properties**. Click **Sorting.** Click **Add** and choose **Category.** Click **Add** again and choose **MonthNo**. Figure 7.23 shows how the dialog box should look.

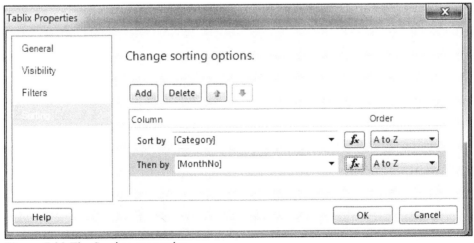

Figure 7.23 The Sorting properties.

Click **OK**. Now if you preview the report, you will see how the order of the data displayed has changed. To allow the end user to sort the data dynamically, go back to Design view. Right-click the **Category** column header and choose **Text Box Properties** as shown in Figure 7.24.

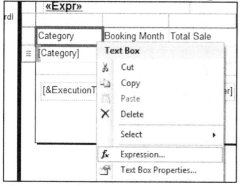

Figure 7.24 Right-click Category.

Select **Interactive Sorting**. Check **Enable interactive sorting on this text box**. Choose **Category** under **Sort by**, as shown in Figure 7.25.

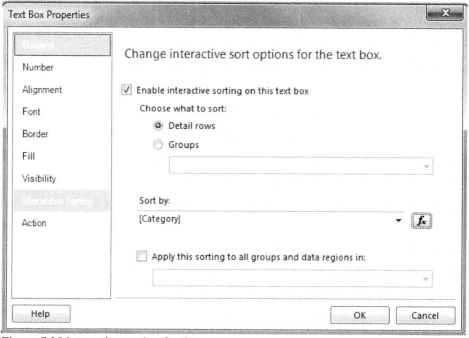

Figure 7.25 Interactive sorting for Category.

Now repeat the process for the **Booking Month** column and sort by the **MonthNo** field. When you run the report, you can now decide how you want the report to sort, either by Category or Month and either ascending or descending.

Click-through Reports

One of the nicest features of Reporting Services is the ability to create click-through reports. This allows the end user to click a cell on the report and drill through to another report that usually shows additional detail. In this section you will learn how to set this up.

Begin by making sure that you have created both of the reports from the Create the Reports section of this chapter. Open the Sales Summary report in Design view. Right-click the **TotalSale** data cell and select **Text Box Properties**. Click **Action**. From the list of possible actions, select **Go to report**. Under **Specify a report**, choose **Sales Details**. The dialog box should look like Figure 7.26 at this point.

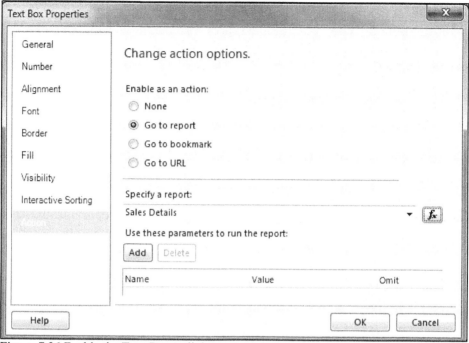

Figure 7.26 Enable the Text Box to link to a report.

The Sales Detail report requires three parameters: Year, Category and Month. You will have to map values from the Sales Summary report that will be passed through to the Sales Detail report. Click **Add** three times and configure the parameters as shown in Figure 7.27. *Do not* click **OK** at this point.

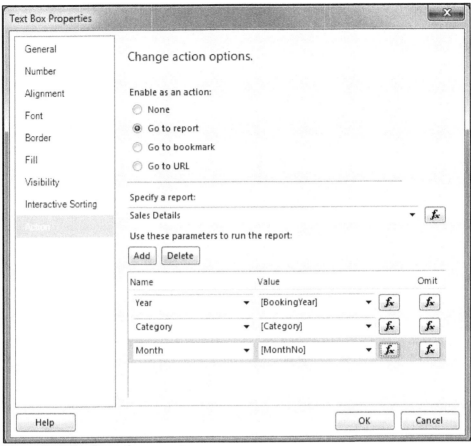

Figure 7.27 Configure the parameters.

The next step is to make sure that the end user knows that the cell is clickable. Click the **Font** page. Change the **Effects** setting to **Underline** (Figure 7.28). This will be a visual clue that the cell is clickable.

137

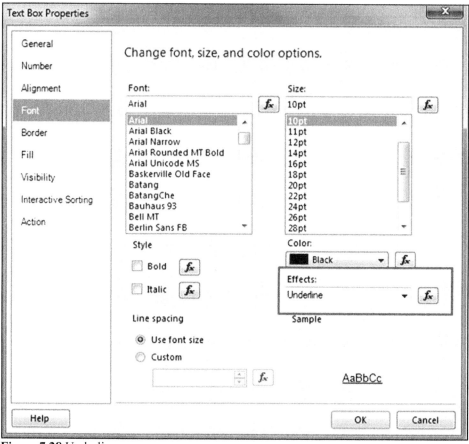

Figure 7.28 Underline.

Click **OK** and now run the report. Click any of the underlined cells to take you to the Sales Details report. There are some enhancements you can make to the detail report to make it look better. Since the end user will get to the report by clicking through from the summary report, you can hide the parameters on the detail report. To do so, go to Design view of the Sales Detail report and find the **Parameters** in the **Report Data** window. Change the **Select parameter visibility** to **Hidden** on the properties of each of the parameters. Since the Sales Details report will run by clicking through from the Sales Summary report, the user doesn't have to specify the parameters for that report. Figure 7.29 shows how to hide parameters.

138

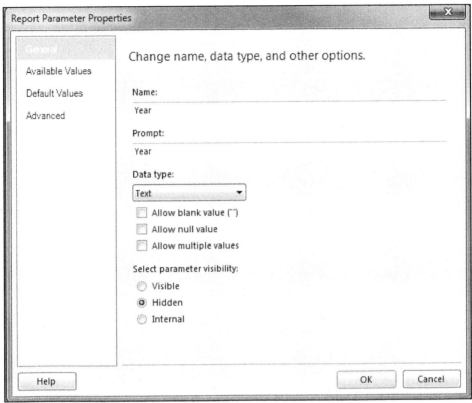

Figure 7.29 Change parameter to hidden.

You might also want to display the parameter values on the detail report to make it more useful. Since this report has three parameters, you might want to create three separate Text Boxes displaying the parameters.

Add three Text Boxes to the header of the report. You may have to increase the height of the header or adjust the position of the title. Right-click the first Text Box and select **Expressions**. In the expression area you will see an equals sign (=). Click next to it and type **"Year: " &**. Now click **Parameters** under **Category**. In the **Values** list, double-click **Year**. The expression should look like Figure 7.30.

139

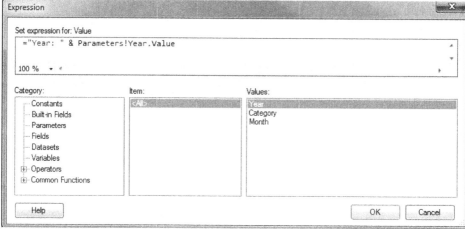

Figure 7.30 The Year parameter expression.

Repeat the process for **Category** in the second Text Box. When you get to the third Text Box, the expression should look like Figure 7.31.

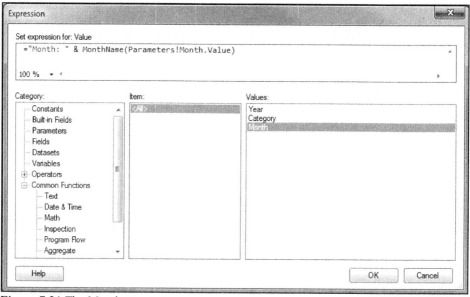

Figure 7.31 The Month parameter.

This expression took advantage of one of the built-in functions available with Reporting Services, the **MonthName** function. While an in depth look at expressions is beyond the scope of this book, feel free to experiment creating your own expressions.

Preview the Sales Summary report and click-through to view the Sales Detail report. Adjust the position and size of the parameter information Text Boxes as needed.

One more feature that would make the detail report better is a link clicking back to the summary report. In Design view of the Sales Detail report, add a Text Box to the header. Type in **Back to Sales Summary** as the value of the Text Box. Make sure that the Text Box has the **Underline** property enabled. Right-click and choose **Text Box Properties**. Select **Action**. Click **Go to report** and select the **Sales Summary** report from the list. The properties should look like Figure 7.32 at this point.

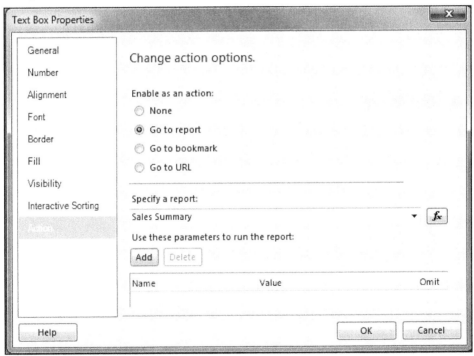

Figure 7.32 Go to the Sales Summary report.

The Sales Summary report requires the Year parameter which is only part of the detail report by way of a parameter. Click **Add** and select **Year** under **Name**. For the **Value**, click the **fx** button. This brings up the Expression dialog box. Click **Parameters** under **Category** and then double-click **Year**. The expression should be =**Parameters!Year.Value**. Figure 7.33 shows how the dialog box looks once the parameter is mapped.

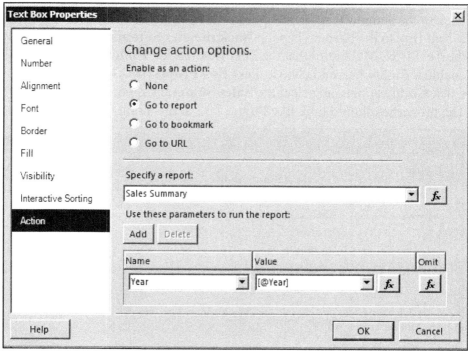

Figure 7.33 Link back to the Sale Summary report.

Click **OK** twice to close both dialog boxes. Now when you are looking at the detail report, you can easily navigate back to the summary report.

Summary

In this chapter you learned how to add dynamic features to your reports making them more user friendly. You will also make the users of your reports happier by giving them some control over how the sorts and the data are displayed.

There is still one more feature to learn about, collapsible/expandable sections. This feature is very similar to the click-through feature, but it requires that all the detail data and summary data are included in one report. You will learn more about this in Chapter 8.

Points to Ponder – Make Your Report Dynamic

1. Make a report dynamic by adding a WHERE clause to the query and letting the user choose values.

2. Parameters are named like this: *@parameter_name*.

3. SSRS will automatically add the parameter to the parameter section based on the query.

4. You can configure the properties of a parameter such as data type, default and available values.

5. You can type in available values or base them on a query.

6. Add hyper-links to the report that click through to a detail report.

7. You can pass parameters to the detail report by mapping fields to parameters.

8. When using parameters, be sure to display the information on the report.

9. You can add interactive sorting so that the end user can choose how to sort the report.

Review Quiz – Chapter Seven

1.)   Why is it a good idea to add dynamic properties to the report?

   O a. To show that you have awesome skills.
   O b. To make the report more complicated.
   O c. To give the end user some control over the data that is displayed on the report.
   O d. To ensure job security.

2.)   Which of the following are possible with SSRS? Choose all that apply.

   O a. A report with cells that the end user can click to go to another report.
   O b. A report with dynamic sorting.
   O c. A report with a parameter list.
   O d. A report with a calendar control to select dates.

Answer Key

1.)   The answer is (c). You should add dynamic properties to make the report better for the end user.

2.)   All of the items listed are possible.

[NOTES]

Chapter 8.   Create a Multi-Level Report

Children's birthday parties, in the US anyway, are very elaborate today. There are swimming parties, bowling parties, rock climbing parties and more. When I was a kid the parties were pretty simple. There was cake and ice cream, pin the tail on the donkey, and presents. Besides demanding that the cake be chocolate with chocolate icing, I wanted a wedding cake for my sixth birthday party. Well, I got the chocolate, but I am pretty sure the cake was just a regular, one or two layer cake baked by my mother.

So far the reports you have built from scratch have been pretty simple with just one level, like my birthday cake. Of course, you have added some nice dynamic features in Chapter 7, but each report has displayed just a detail line for the data. In this chapter you will learn how to create more complex reports with multiple grouping levels.

Add Groups

When you think about data, there are often several pieces of information repeated on multiple rows. For example, multiple sales take place within a year or month or by the same sales person. Instead of repeating this data over and over, SSRS allows you to set up groups on those repeating fields along with subtotals.

The Base Report

Get started by creating a new Report Server Project called **MultiLevel** and save it in the C:\Joes2Pros\SSRSCompanionFiles\Chapter8\Project folder. Create a shared data source called **JProCo** pointing to your local SQL Server instance and the JProCo database. If you need help with these tasks, refer back to the step by step exercises in previous chapters.

Add a new report to the project by right-clicking the **Reports** folder and selecting **Add > New Item**. Make sure to select **Report**, not **Report**

Wizard, and name the report **Employee Sales**. The screen should look like Figure 8.1.

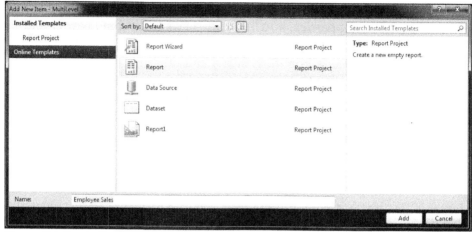

Figure 8.1 Create the Employee Sales report.

Now that you have the new report in place, switch to the **Report Data** window and create a data source pointing to the shared data source. Name it **JProCo**. Create a dataset that uses the new data source and the query found at C:\Joes2Pros\SSRSCompanionFiles\Chapter8\Resources\SalesByEmploye e.sql. Name the dataset **SalesByEmployee**. The dataset should look like Figure 8.2. Be sure to review Chapter 4 if you need to review how to create a data source or dataset.

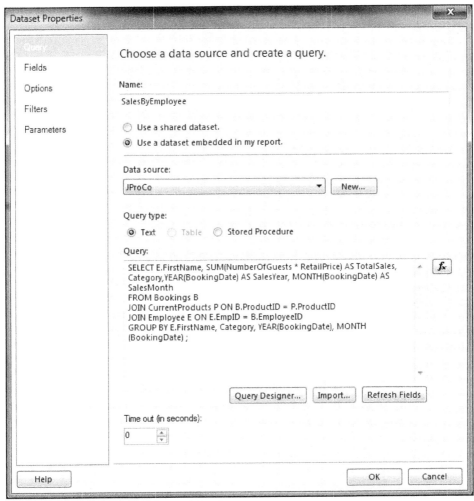

Figure 8.2 The SalesByEmployee dataset.

Double-click the report to open it in Design mode. Select **Add Header** from the Report menu. Select **Add Footer** from the Report menu. Drag a Text Box from the **Toolbox** window to the report header. Change the font of the Text Box to **Tahoma, 20pt, bold** using whatever method you prefer. Change the **Foreground Color** to **Steel Blue**. You'll have to click **More Colors** to find **Steel Blue**. Type **Employee Sales** as the title. Position the Text Box to the left of the header and decrease the height of

149

the header to remove extra space. The report should look like Figure 8.3 at this point.

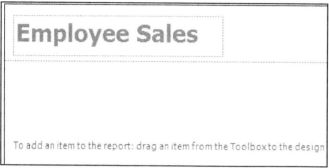

Figure 8.3 The report with report header.

Drag a Table control from the Toolbox to the report body. The Table control will be used to display the data, but you will add the fields in a much different way when creating multiple levels. Start by adding just the **FirstName** and **TotalSale** fields to the report. Make sure that FirstName is on the left and TotalSales is on the right. These two fields will make up the detail line of the report. Delete the extra column. Add an overall total by right-clicking the **TotalSales** cell and choosing **Add Total**. Type **Total** in the cell under **FirstName**. Change the font weight of the overall total row to **Bold** and the font family to **Tahoma**. Add the Execution Time and Page Number to the footer. At this point, the report definition should look like Figure 8.4.

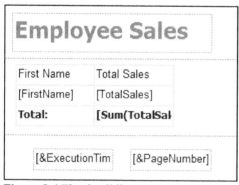

Figure 8.4 The detail line.

Determine Grouping Hierarchy

Take a look at the fields available for the report. After using FirstName and TotalSales for the detail, there are three fields that you will group on in this report: **SalesYear**, **SalesMonth**, and **Category**. When deciding the order of adding the groups, you have to determine if there are any hierarchies in the data. In this case, SalesYear is a parent to SalesMonth.

Category doesn't relate to either of the other fields. Therefore, you would have the choice of making Category the outermost group or the innermost group. In your job, you would ask questions of the person who requested the report to determine where Category fits on the report. For this report, you will add Category as the innermost group. The grouping hierarchy for this report will be **SalesYear > SalesMonth > Category > Detail**.

Add the Groups

There are quite a few options when adding groups. You can add header and footer rows, sorting and more. To start, right-click on the detail row. Select **Add Group > Row Group > Parent Group** (Figure 8.5).

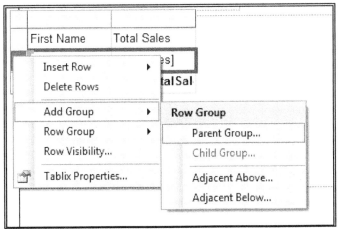

Figure 8.5 Add a parent group.

This will bring up the **Tablix group** dialog box. Select **Category** in the **Group by** dropdown box and check **Add group header**. Figure 8.6 shows the dialog box.

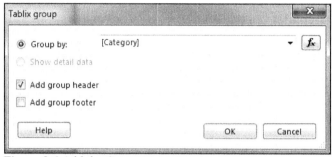

Figure 8.6 Add the Category group.

Click **OK**. Right-click the **Category** row to add another parent group, but this time select the **SalesMonth** field with a group header. Finally, right-click the **SalesMonth** row and add the **SalesYear** parent group. Figure 8.7 shows how the report design should look after adding the groups.

Figure 8.7 The report after adding groups.

Add Subtotals

The next step is to add subtotals for each grouping level. SSRS makes this really easy. In each of the cells under the Total Sales heading that is blank,

152

hover the cursor over the right side of the cell until you see the icon with the list of fields. Choose **TotalSales** in each case. SSRS will automatically change to the **[Sum(TotalSales)]** expression. Format all of the **TotalSales** cells as currency with zero decimal places and use the 1000 separator. Align the entire column to the right. The report design should look like Figure 8.8.

Employee Sales

Sales Year	Sales Month	Category	First Name	Total Sales
[SalesYear]				ım(TotalSales)]
	[SalesMonth]			ım(TotalSales)]
		[Category]		ım(TotalSales)]
			[FirstName]	[TotalSales]
			Total:	**n(TotalSales)]**

Figure 8.8 The report with subtotals.

Go ahead and preview the report (Figure 8.9). At this point the data is there, however, you still have some work to do to make this report look nice.

Employee Sales

Sales Year	Sales Month	Category	First Name	Total Sales
2006				$314,645
	1			$31,169
		LongTerm-Stay		$27,173
			Eric	$6,752
			Lee	$17,232
			Sally	$3,189
		No-Stay		$652
			Sally	$652
		Overnight-Stay		$3,344
			Barbara	$2,519
			Lisa	$258
			Terry	$567
	2			$17,814
		LongTerm-Stay		$9,870

Figure 8.9 The report preview.

Take a look at the bottom of the report in Design view. You should see the grouping information. If you can't see it, select **Grouping Window** from the **Report > View** menu. This report has four grouping levels.

Format the Groups

The first thing that would make the report look better is to change the **SalesMonth** to the name of the month instead of the number. To do this, make sure the report is in Design view. Right-click on the **SalesMonth** column and choose **Expression**. Click to the right of the equal sign (=) in the **Expression** dialog box. Under **Category** expand **Common Functions** and click **Date & Time**. In the **Item** list, double-click **MonthName**. Add

154

a close parentheses to the end of the expression. The expression should look like Figure 8.10.

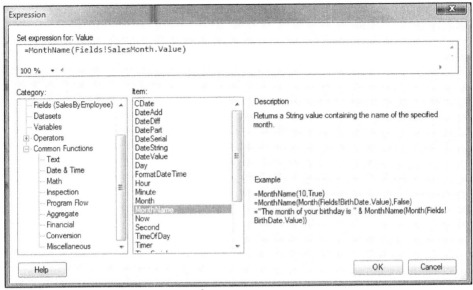

Figure 8.10 The MonthName expression.

Click **OK**. Now you will add some color and formatting to the report data. As you have seen there are three ways to change the formatting of a cell. You can also change the properties of an entire row or column at once when using the **Properties** window. Select the top row which has the headings. Hit **F4** to open the **Properties** window. Now when you modify a property it will affect every cell.

Table 8.1 Table 8.1 has the properties for you to change for each row.

Property	Heading	SalesYear	SalesMonth	Category	FirstName
Background Color	Steel Blue	#6e9eca	Slate Gray	#8fa0b0	No color
Color	White	White	White	White	Black
FontFamily	Tahoma	Tahoma	Tahoma	Tahoma	Tahoma
FontSize	11pt	10pt	10pt	10pt	10pt
FontStyle	Default	Default	Default	Default	Default
FontWeight	Bold	Bold	Bold	Bold	Default

Preview the report. It should look like Figure 8.11.

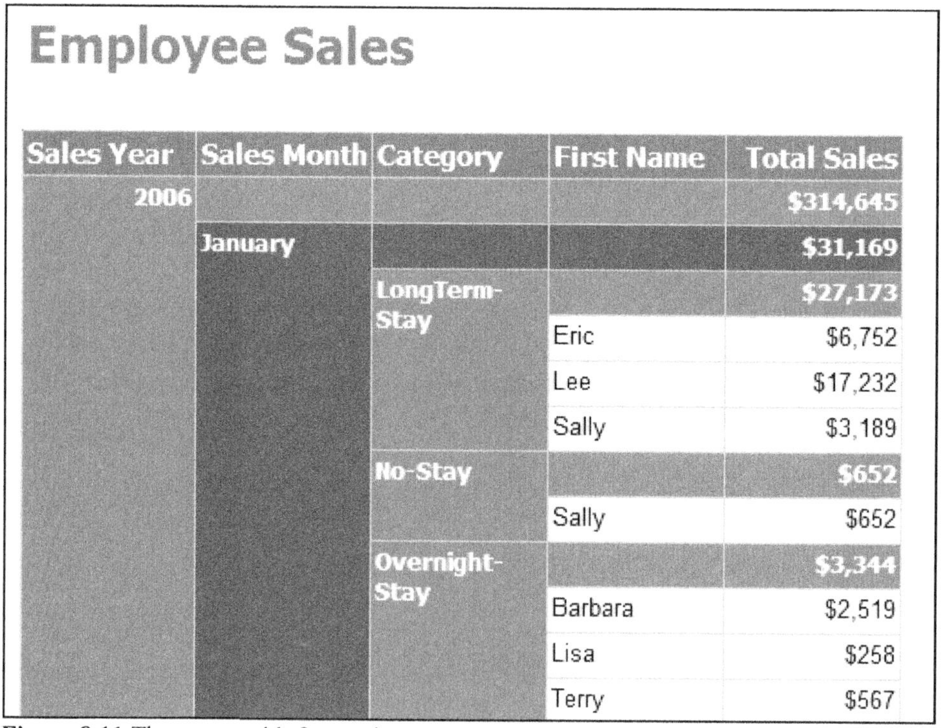

Employee Sales

Sales Year	Sales Month	Category	First Name	Total Sales
2006				$314,645
	January			$31,169
		LongTerm-Stay		$27,173
			Eric	$6,752
			Lee	$17,232
			Sally	$3,189
		No-Stay		$652
			Sally	$652
		Overnight-Stay		$3,344
			Barbara	$2,519
			Lisa	$258
			Terry	$567

Figure 8.11 The report with formatting.

There is still a problem with the report. If you page through the report, you will see that the headings disappear. To keep them visible on each page, click the small arrow on the upper right side of the **Grouping** window and choose **Advanced Mode**. This makes the static sections visible. Figure 8.12 shows where to find this setting.

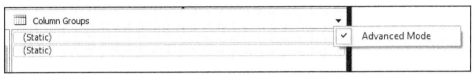

Figure 8.12 Turn on Advanced Mode.

Select the top **Static** section under **Column Groups**. In the Properties window, change the **RepeatOnNewPage** property to **True**. Now when you page through the report, the headings stay in place. You can turn off the Advanced Mode when you are in Design mode again.

Collapsing Sections

In Chapter 7 you learned about several dynamic features that you can add to reports. One feature was purposely left out because it only applies to reports with groups. To get started, make sure you can see the **Group** window. Right-click the **SalesMonth** group in **Row Groups** and choose **Group Properties**. Click **Visibility**. Select **Hide**. Check **Display can be toggled by this report item**. Choose **SalesYear** from the dropdown box. Figure 8.13 shows how this looks.

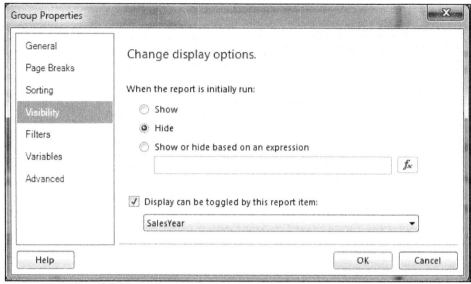

Figure 8.13 The Visibility properties.

READER NOTE: By default, the Text Boxes are named the same as the fields you add. However, if you make a change, the name of the Text Box does not change. If you do not see the correct item in the list, you can change the Text Box's name in the Name property found in the Properties window.

Repeat this process so that the Category group toggles by the SalesMonth Text Box and the Details group toggles by the Category Text Box. Preview the report. The report should look like Figure 8.14.

Employee Sales

Sales Year	Sales Month	Category	First Name	Total Sales
⊞ 2006				$314,645
⊞ 2007				$351,831
⊞ 2008				$350,233
⊞ 2009				$390,409
⊞ 2010				$309,976
⊞ 2011				$374,136
⊞ 2012				$349,481
⊞ 2013				$309,500
			Total:	$2,750,211

Figure 8.14 The report with the groups collapsed.

Expand the sections to see the child groups and details. You may or may not like this feature. In the past, I have rarely used it. My customers have either wanted all the groups and details displayed or the ability to click through to a detail report.

Sorting

Just as you can sort the data displayed in a table, you can also sort the grouping levels. In this case, when reviewing the group properties, Reporting Services has automatically added the grouping field to the sorting properties. For example, assume that you wanted to view the report with the latest sales data first. In the **Grouping** window at the bottom of the screen, right-click the **SalesYear** level and choose **Group Properties**. Click **Sorting**. And then change the **Order** to **Z to A**. Click **OK**. Repeat the process on the SalesMonth group.

Now when you preview the report, the data will be displayed in descending order.

Create a Matrix Report

Matrix reports give you the ability to twist or pivot the data. For example, you might need to create a report that displays the years or months as column headers.

In the next example, you will create a report that displays the employee names as column headers. Figure 8.15 shows how the report will look when it is complete.

Category	Month	Alex	Barbara	Barry	David	Eric	James	John	Lee	Lisa	Sally	Terry
LongTerm-Stay			$2,623	$8,016	$13,566	$22,638	$16,602	$8,747	$45,036	$37,554	$18,089	
	January					6,752			17,232		3,189	
	February					9,870						
	March		2,623	664	5,241					4,682		
	April			1,992			12,731					
	May				6,016							
	June								4,265			
	July			7,352								

Figure 8.15 The matrix report.

READER NOTE: The term Tablix is a combination of Table and Matrix. It is possible to start with a table and add column groups to turn it into a matrix.

Create the Matrix Report

To get started, create a new report in the MultiLevel project called **Employee Matrix.** Add a data source to the report called **JProCo** that points to the shared data source. Create a dataset called **EmpoyeeBookings** that uses the JProCo data source. Import the query found at C:\Joes2Pros\SSRSCompanionFiles\Chapter8\Resources\EmployeeMatrix .sql file. Be sure to review previous examples in this book if you need help with these tasks.

From the Toolbox, drag a matrix control to the report design canvas. The grid for the matrix is different than the Table control you have worked with so far. Figure 8.16 shows how the Matrix control looks.

Figure 8.16 The matrix grid.

Click the edge of the **Columns** cell so that the list of fields displays. Select **FirstName**. Select **TotalSales** in the **Data** cell and **SalesMonth** in the **Rows** cell. The grid should now look like Figure 8.17.

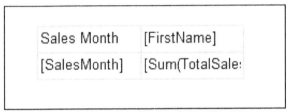

Figure 8.17 The matrix with the fields filled in.

While matrix reports are more complex than regular table reports, they are not difficult to create. The most difficult aspect is figuring out what to put where. The Columns cell is the information that you want displayed as column headings across the top of the report. For example, in this report, the actual employee first names become column headings. The Data cell holds the non-grouping level data. It is usually numeric data and will be aggregated in some way, typically using the SUM function. The Rows cell holds the traditional grouping level field where you want the field name at the top of the report with the data underneath. In this example, the field name, Sales Month, is displayed as the heading with the actual months listed below it.

Preview the report and type **2006** for the **Year** parameter. The report should look something like Figure 8.18.

Sales Month	Alex	Barbara	Barry	David	Eric	James	John
1		2518.5006			6752.0250		
2					9870.3850		
3	418.0248	6678.1740	663.9750	8571.5364		293.2980	
4		853.7040	2551.1640	1991.9250	6738.2688	12731.1210	2791.9690
5		1154.0340	781.7760		6016.0100		
6		6894.8250	714.8120		672.8832		
7		6138.7380	7352.3520	3603.8796	14642.5960	3715.6372	8156.6640
8			510.5440	756.0180			2443.0500
9	1333.2774		363.8448	6453.0522			
10	564.5360					6197.6120	9169.0320
11	6566.8204				262.0512	2903.3280	
12		1012.8170	412.1550	5021.0280			2008.4112

Figure 8.18 The matrix report.

Go back to Design view and add another Row group by right-clicking the bottom row and selecting **Add Group** > **Row Group** > **Parent Group**, as shown in Figure 8.19.

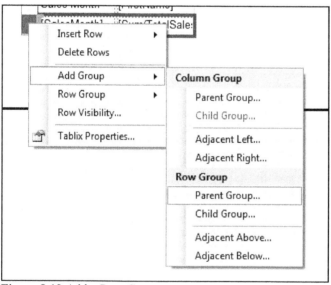

Figure 8.19 Add a Row Group.

Select **SalesMonth** and add a group header. The dialog box should look like Figure 8.20.

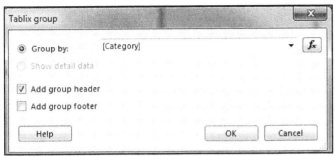

Figure 8.20 Create the Category group.

After clicking **OK**, the report design should look like Figure 8.21.

Category	Sales Month	[FirstName]
[Category]		
	[SalesMonth]	[Sum(TotalSale:

Figure 8.21 The report design with the Category group.

Instead of displaying the month number, the report would look better with the month name instead. Right-click on the **SalesMonth** cell and choose **Expression**. Set the expression as **=MonthName(Fields!SalesMonth.Value)** and click **OK**. To display a subtotal for the Category groups, add the **TotalSales** field to the empty cell under **FirstName**.

It is also possible to add additional column groups, but this is something I have rarely done in practice. You also need to make sure that there are not too many distinct values in the column group because the report can become too wide very quickly.

Format the Report

The report displays the data, but it is still very plain. To make the report more attractive for the end users you will add some color and highlighting. The matrix report is easy to format, and it is done by cell instead of by group. To format more than one cell at a time, hold down the **Control** key to select the cells, then use the **Properties** window to set the formatting properties. Figure 8.22 shows the areas to format according to Table 8.2.

Modify the report cells using the settings found in Table 8.2 and the areas shown in Figure 8.22. All cells are Arial 10 pt.

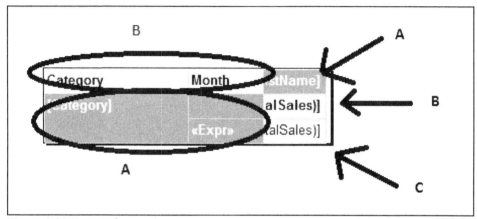

Figure 8.22 How to format the report.

Table 8.2

Area	Background Color	Font Color	Font Weight
A	*#6e9eca*	White	Bold
B	White	Black	Bold
C	White	Black	Default

Make sure that the **TotalSales** cells are formatted for currency and the entire column is right-aligned. Adjust the column widths as needed. Preview the report to see how it looks.

Normally, you would add some additional enhancements such as a report title and a parameter list. You will continue working on this report in Chapter 9.

Create a Subreport

You can fulfill many report requirements using the Table and Matrix controls. Occasionally, you will run into a situation that doesn't quite fit these models. One solution that often works is using a subreport. A subreport is a separate report that is embedded inside a cell of the main report. This technique is often used to combine data from datasets that come from different database servers. In the following example, you will display the total sales by year and month along with a list of the sales people who did *not* have sales that month.

To get started, add a new report to the project called **Sales Summary**. The report's data source will point to the JProCo shared data source. Create a dataset called SalesSummary based on the file found at C:\Joes2Pros\SSRSCompanionFiles\Chapter8\Resources\SalesSummary.sql.

Drag a Table control to the report canvas and add the **SalesMonth** and **TotalSales** fields to the table. Delete the empty column. Right-click on **SalesMonth** and select **Add Group > Row Group > Parent Group.** Select the **SalesYear** field for the grouping level and add a group header. Add a title, **Sales Summary**, to the header and add ExecutionTime and PageNumber fields to the footer. The report definition should look like Figure 8.23.

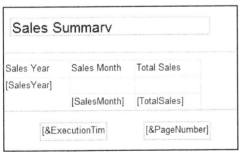

Figure 8.23 The Sales Summary report definition.

Preview the report to make sure it runs. It should look like Figure 8.24.

165

Sales Summary

Sales Year	Sales Month	Total Sales
2006		
	1	31168.6684
	2	17814.3170
	3	24258.5742
	4	27865.1878
	5	11955.8384
	6	14776.6302
	7	44133.9692
	8	13815.1620
	9	34202.7824
	10	41345.2390
	11	40353.0256
	12	12955.6862
2007		
	1	27136.7714

Figure 8.24 The Sales Summary Report.

Now you will create a second report that will be used as a subreport. Name the second report **SalesSummarySubReport**. Create a data source pointing to the JProCo shared data source. Create a dataset named **EmployeeNoSales** by importing the C:\Joes2Pros\SSRSCompanionFiles\Chapter8\Resources\SubReport.sql file.

Drag a Table control to the report and add the **EmpID**, **LastName**, and **FirstName** fields to the table. Select the header row and change the font weight to **Bold**. Make sure the table is in the upper right corner of the design canvas. Drag the right and bottom edges of the report so that they fit against the edges of the table removing and extra space. The report design should look like Figure 8.25.

Emp ID	Last Name	First Name
[EmpID]	[LastName]	[FirstName]

Figure 8.25 The subreport definition.

Preview the report to make sure it works entering **2006** for Year and **1** for Month. Figure 8.26 shows how the report should look.

Emp ID	Last Name	First Name
1	Adams	Alex
2	Brown	Barry
4	Kennson	David
7	Lonning	David
8	Marshbank	John
9	Newton	James

Figure 8.26 The subreport preview.

Now go back to the Sales Summary report and open it in Design view. To add the subreport, you will need to add an additional two rows to the report. Right-click the bottom row and select **Insert Row > Below**. Repeat to add the second row. Select the two cells under the **SalesMonth** and **TotalSales** cells at once by holding down the **SHIFT** key. Right-click and select **Merge Cells**. This will change the two cells into one wider cell. Repeat the process with two cells directly beneath the wide cell you just created.

In the first wide cell, type in **Employees with no sales** and change the font weight to **Bold**. Change the text alignment to **Center**. At this point, the table should look like Figure 8.27.

Sales Year	Sales Month	Total Sales
[SalesYear]		
	[SalesMonth]	[TotalSales]
	Employees with no sales	

Figure 8.27 The table with two wide cells.

From the Toolbox, drag a **Subreport** control to the bottom cell. Right-click the **Subreport** and select **Subreport Properties**. On the **General** page, select **SaleSummarySubReport** under **Use this report as a subreport**. Since the data that should display on the subreport depends on the year and month, click **Parameter**s. On this page you will map the parameters from the main report to the subreport. Click **Add** and select **Year** under **Name** and **[SalesYear]** under **Value**. The dialog box should look like Figure 8.28.

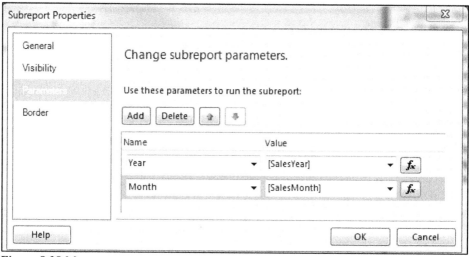

Figure 8.28 Map parameters.

Click **OK**. Preview the report. Under each month, you will see a list of sales people who did not contribute to the sales for that month. Figure 8.29 shows how the report should look.

Sales Summary

Sales Year	Sales Month			Total Sales
2006				
		1		31168.6684
	Employees with no sales			
	Emp ID	**Last Name**	**First Name**	
	1	Adams	Alex	
	2	Brown	Barry	
	4	Kennson	David	
	7	Lonning	David	
	8	Marshbank	John	
	9	Newton	James	
		2		17814.3170

Figure 8.29 The Sales Summary preview.

In the next chapter you will learn about another reason to use subreports.

Summary

Most reports will contain grouping levels, and many developers find this the most challenging aspect of Reporting Services. Spend some time making sure you understand the report requirements and how the fields relate to each other. Of course, if you mess up the groups, it is easy enough to remove them or even delete the report and start again.

Points to Ponder – Create a Multi-Level Report

1. Your report starts with a Detail level, but you can add one or more parent groups.

2. Multiple levels of groups are nested as parent/child groups.

3. You can add summary values at the group levels.

4. The row groupings are listed on the left at the bottom of the report in the Grouping Window.

5. Right-click on the grouping listed at the bottom to control properties such as sorting.

6. Groups can be expanded and collapsed by the Hide property.

7. A matrix report is a pivot report. Some of the data is moved up as column headings.

8. A good field to pivot is the Year or Month field.

9. A matrix report has COLUMN groupings and can also have ROW groupings.

10. Subreports can be added at the detail level of a report.

11. Link a value from the main report to the parameter of the subreport.

Review Quiz – Chapter Eight

1.)   Which statement is true?

    O a. Grouping levels are really difficult to learn, so you should just change the report requirements.

    O b. A Matrix report can only have column groups.

    O c. Most reports have grouping levels.

    O d. Only one Row group can be added per report.

2.)   How do you find the group properties?

    O a. Right-click on the group's row and choose Properties.

    O b. Right-click on the group in the Group Window.

Answer Key

1.)   Answer (a) is not correct. With practice you will become proficient with groups. Answer (b) is not correct because Matrix reports can have column and row level groups. Answer (d) is not correct. You can have many grouping levels in a report. Answer (c) is the correct answer.

2.)   The best way to view the group properties is by right-clicking on the group name in the Group Window, so answer (b) is correct.

[NOTES]

Chapter 9.   Add Visual Appeal

They say a picture is worth a thousand words. When it comes to Reporting Services, a picture is also worth a thousand numbers. With just a glance at charts, graphs, gauges, and maps, it is possible to know if the salespeople have met their quotas, inventory levels or how the company is doing. It is sometimes joked that the higher the pay grade, the more pictures are required on the report.

Reporting Services has a rich set of features for displaying information visually. In this chapter you will learn how to add these elements to your reports by building the dashboard report from Chapter 2.

Working with Charts and Graphs

The most basic visual element you can add to a report is a chart. A chart displays information comparing two data points, for example, a bar chart showing the sales for each year. A graph is very similar to a chart, but usually shows a trend represented by a line instead of bars. There are also other types of charts, like pie charts. You can combine charts and graphs to compare different types of information. Figure 9.1 shows an example of a combination chart and graph.

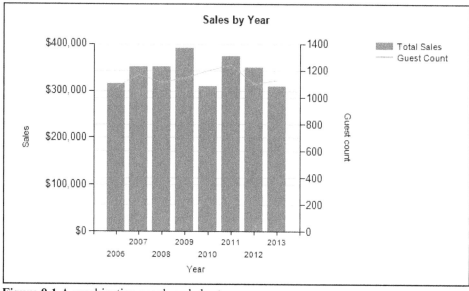

Figure 9.1 A combination graph and chart.

Add a Chart to a Report

To get started, create a new project called **Visual** in the C:\Joes2Pros\SSRSCompanionFiles\Chapter9\Project folder. Set up a shared data source pointing to your local SQL Server instance and the JProCo database. Add a new report called **Chart**. Create a data source pointing to the shared data source. Create a dataset named **SalesByMonth**. Base the dataset on the SalesByMonth.sql file found at C:\Joes2Pros\SSRSCompanionFiles\Chapter9\Resources.

From the Toolbox, drag a Chart control to the report design canvas. Instead of seeing the control on the report, this action brings up a dialog box (Figure 9.2) where you will select the type of chart you wish to use.

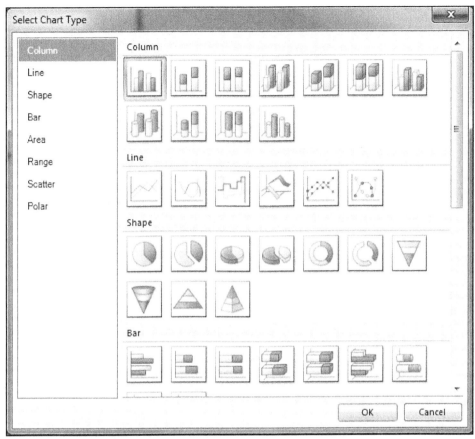

Figure 9.2 Select a chart type.

Select the very first type, the **Column** type, and click **OK**. Figure 9.3 shows the control before any of the properties are configured.

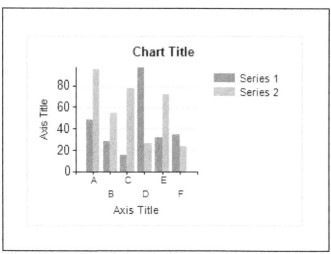

Figure 9.3 The chart before configuring properties.

Drag the chart to the upper leftmost corner of the report. Turn on the report ruler and change the size of the chart to 5 inches wide by 2.5 inches high or 13 cm wide by 6.5 inches tall. Change the **Chart Title** to **Sales by Month** by clicking into the text and typing. Change the vertical **Axis Title** (y axis) to **Sales** and the horizontal **Axis Title** (x axis) to **Month**.

Click the series titles and a new window will pop up where you will configure the data for the chart. Click the plus sign next to Values and select **TotalSales**. Under **Category Groups**, change the values **Details** to **SalesMonth**. Figure 9.4 shows how the Chart Data should look.

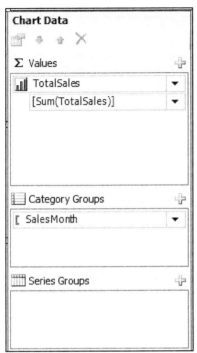

Figure 9.4 The Chart Data properties.

Click anywhere on the report design canvas to close the Chart Data window and see the results. Figure 9.5 shows how the chart looks in Design view.

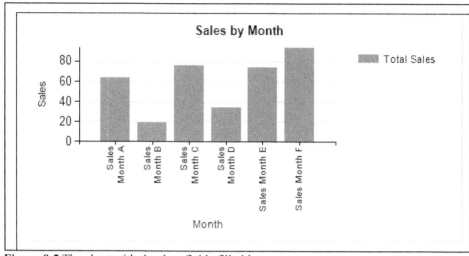

Figure 9.5 The chart with the data fields filled in.

Preview the report and type in **2006** for the Year parameter to see how it looks at this point as shown in Figure 9.6.

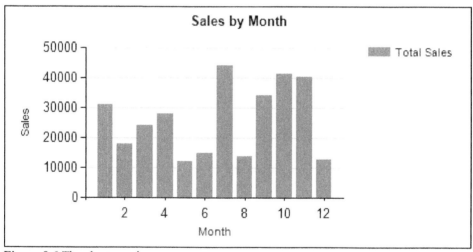

Figure 9.6 The chart preview.

The Sales numbers would look better formatted as currency. Back in Design view, right-click the vertical axis and select **Vertical Axis Properties**. Click **Number** and **Currency**. Set **Decimal Places** to zero and check **Use 1000 separator**. Now when you preview the report, it should look like Figure 9.7.

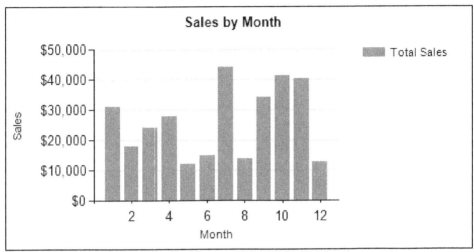

Figure 9.7 The formatted chart with data.

A chart can display multiple data points as long as they come from the same dataset. In this case, the data has totals for the currently displayed year and the year previous to the currently displayed year so they can be compared. To set this up, go back to Design view and click **Total Sales** to bring up the **Chart Data** window. Click the plus sign next to **Values** and select **PreviousYearSales**. By default, the chart will display a yellow column for this new data next to the blue column. Change this to a line by clicking **PreviousYearSales** and selecting **Change Chart Type**. Figure 9.8 shows where to find this.

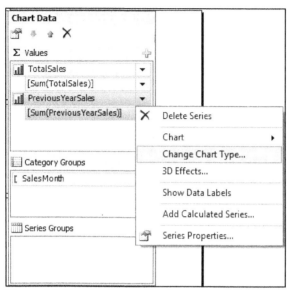

Figure 9.8 How to change the chart type.

When the Select Chart Type dialog pops up, select the 3D Line type. This changes the entire chart to 3-D. Preview the report, but make sure to type in a year after 2006, such as 2007 in order to display the previous year's data.

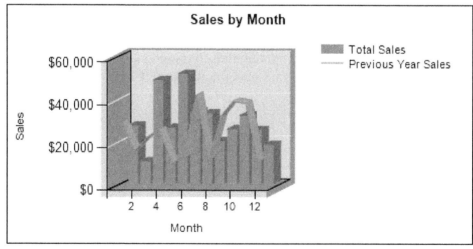

Figure **9.9** shows the chart.

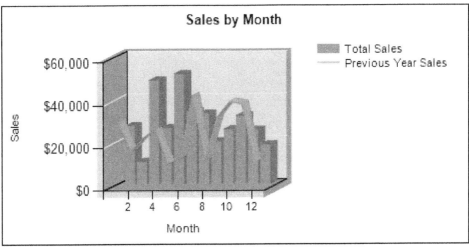

Figure 9.9 The 3-D chart.

Add a Pie Chart to a Report

As you probably noticed, there are several chart types you can add to an SSRS report. In this section, you will add a pie chart that breaks down the sales by category.

Begin by adding a second dataset named **SalesByCategory** to the report. Base the dataset on the query from SalesByCategory.sql file found in the C:\Joes2Pros\SSRSCompanionFiles\Chapter9\Resources folder. Drag a second chart control to the report design surface. This time select the **3-D Pie** shape from the **Select Chart Type** dialog box. Line the chart up with the first chart and drag the right edge until the report is 9.5 inches or 24 cm wide. The height should match the height of the first chart.

Click the category legend area to open the **Chart Data** window. Click the plus sign next to **Values**. This time, since there are two datasets, you must not only select the field, you must also select the dataset. Choose **TotalSales** from the **SalesByCategory** dataset as shown in Figure 9.10.

181

Figure 9.10 Find the TotalSales from SalesByCategory.

While the Chart Data window is still displayed, change the **Category Groups** from **Details** to **Category**. The Chart Data window should look like Figure 9.11.

Figure 9.11 The Chart Data window.

Change the **Chart Title** to **Sales by Category**. Preview the report. Figure 9.12 shows the report.

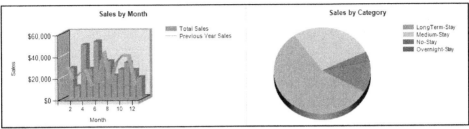

Figure 9.12 The report with both charts.

One final touch to add to these charts is a tooltip. This allows the end user to mouse over sections of the charts and see more information. Change back to Design view and right-click on one of the blue columns. Select **Series Properties**. Click **Series Data**. Click the expression button (**fx**) under **Tooltip** to bring up the **Expression** dialog box. Type in the formula **=FormatCurrency(Fields!TotalSales.Value)** and click **OK** twice. Repeat the process with the yellow line and the formula **=FormatCurrency(Fields!PreviousYearSales.Value)**. Repeat the process once more with the pie chart and the formula **=Fields!Category.Value + ": " + FormatCurrency(Fields!TotalSales.Value)**. Preview the report and make sure the tooltips work.

Complete the Dashboard

Dashboard type reports generally contain one or more charts plus a way to drill down to view more detailed data. Reporting Services lends itself very well to dashboards, but there is one problem. The table and matrix controls will expand to accommodate the data, which can affect the placement of these and other controls. To see this problem, you will add the matrix you created in Chapter 8 to this report.

Import the Employee Matrix report you created in Chapter 8 to the project by right-clicking on the **Reports** folder found in the Solution Explorer and choosing **Add > Existing Item**. If you created the matrix report in the previous chapter, navigate to the C:\Joes2Pros\SSRSCompanionFiles\Chapter8\Project\MultiLevel\MultiLe vel folder and select Employee Matrix.rdl file. If you did not create the report, you can find it in the Resources folder for Chapter 9.

Double-click the **Employee Matrix** report to open it up in Design view. Make sure that the **Sales Month** group is set to collapse by right-clicking the **SalesMonth** group found in the **Row Groups**. Click **Visibility** and select **Hide**. Check **Display can be toggled by this report item** and select **Category** from the list. Click **OK**.

Click the matrix so that column and row handles appear. Right-click the small square at the intersection of the column and row handles and select **Copy**. Switch to the Chart report and **Paste** under the two charts. Move the matrix to the left side of the report and right under the charts. Figure 9.13 shows how the Chart report should look with the matrix added to it.

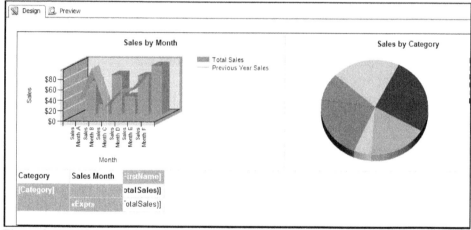

Figure 9.13 Add the matrix to the Chart report.

Add a third dataset to the Chart report based on the query in the EmployeeMatrix.sql file found at C:\Joes2Pros\SSRSCompanionFiles\Chapter9\Resources. Name the dataset **EmployeeBookings**.

READER NOTE: *If you get an error stating that the Tablix refers to an invalid dataset, you may have a mismatch in how the dataset was named* *in the original report and this one. To fix this, change the* **DataSetName** *property found in the Properties window of the matrix.*

When previewing the report (Figure 9.14) you will see that the matrix expanded, causing the pie chart to move drastically to the right. To fix this problem, you will add the chart and matrix reports as subreports to a main report. This prevents one area of the report from interfering with another area.

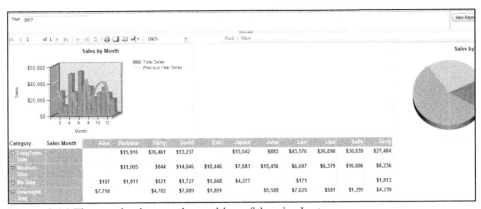

Figure 9.14 The matrix changes the position of the pie chart.

To begin, remove the matrix from the Chart report. Then drag the edges of the report so that they fit right up against the charts removing all white space. Also delete the **EmployeeSales** dataset. Open up the **Employee Matrix** report in Design view. Drag the edges of the report to remove any extra space in that report as well.

Add a new report to the project named **Dashboard**. The Dashboard report will just be a container for the other two reports, but it must pass a parameter to those two reports. To do so, the Dashboard report must also have a parameter.

Begin by creating a data source pointing to the JProCo shared data source. Create a dataset called **SalesYear** based on the query in the YearParameter.sql file found at C:\Joes2Pros\SSRSCompanionFiles\Chapter9\Resources.

185

Right-click the **Parameters** folder found in the **Report Data** window and select **Add Parameter**. Name the parameter **Year** and change the **Prompt** value to **Year** as well. Click **Available Values** and select **Get values from a query**. Select **SalesYear** for the **Dataset**. Select **BookingYear** for both the **Value field** and **Label field**. Figure 9.15 shows how these properties should look.

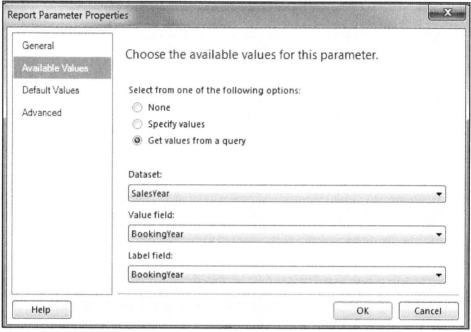

Figure 9.15 The Available Values properties.

Click **Default Values** and select **Specify values**. Click **Add** and fill in the value **2012**. Click **OK** to accept the parameter properties. Figure 9.16 shows how the Default Values screen should look.

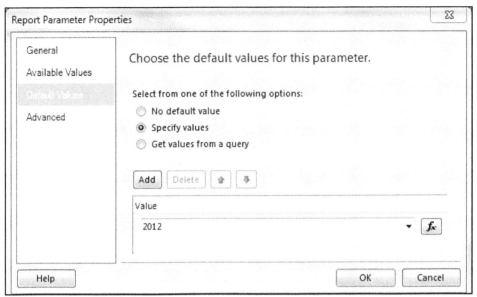

Figure 9.16 The Default Values.

Click **OK**. Now that the parameter is in place, drag two Subreport controls to the report placing one above the other and lined up on the left. Right-click the top subreport and select **Subreport Properties**. Choose the **Chart** report as the **Use this report as a subreport** property. Figure 9.17 shows the General page.

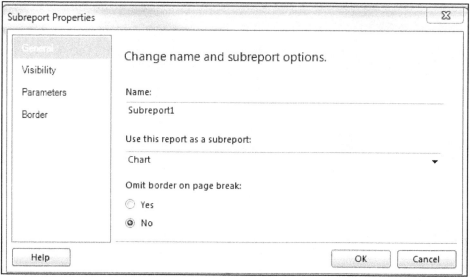

Figure 9.17 Set up the subreport.

Click **Parameters**. Click **Add** and select **Year** for the **Name**. Under **Value**, there is nothing in the list except for a formula grabbing the first year in our parameter list. This is not helpful at all. If we select this, then the year will always equal 2006 regardless of what the end user has chosen. Instead, click the expression button (**fx**). If anything is in the **Expression** window, remove it and replace it with the expression **=Parameters!Year.Value**. An easy way to create this expression is to type in the equal sign, then click **Parameters** and double-click **Year**. By setting the value in this way, the year that the end user selects will be passed to the subreport.

Once the expression is complete, click **OK** to dismiss the **Expression** window and again to dismiss the **Subreport Properties**. Repeat this process with the second subreport. This subreport will point to the **Employee Matrix** report. Don't forget to map the parameter.

Preview the dashboard. It already looks much better!

Add Images to Reports

The dashboard is almost complete, but it is lacking a title. You may want to come up with a standard heading including a logo for all reports. Open the dashboard report in Design view. Add a header by clicking **Report > Add Page Header**. In the **Report Data** window, right-click **Images** and select **Add Image**. Navigate to the JProCo.jpg file found in the C:\Joes2Pros\SSRSCompanionFiles\Chapter9\Resources folder and click **Open**. Drag the JProCo image from the **Images** folder to the report header. This will bring up a Properties dialog box. Click **OK** to dismiss the dialog box. The image can now be seen on the report, but it is very small. Expand the size so that it is about the same height as the header.

In addition to images, you can also add lines to an SSRS report. Drag a line from the Toolbox to the header of the report. Make sure that it is perfectly horizontal and expand to the width of the report going over the logo. The report header should look like Figure 9.18 at this point.

Figure 9.18 The report header.

Open the Properties window and select the line. Change the color to **Blue** and the width to **15pt**. With the line selected, click **Format > Order > Send to Back**. This will move the line behind the logo. Adjust the image and line as needed.

Add a Text Box to the area above the line and to the right of the logo. Add this expression to the Text Box: =**"Joes 2 Pros Sales Dashboard for " & Parameters!Year.Value**. Expand the width of the Text Box and change the color to **Blue** and the font size to **16pt** and **Bold** weight. Expand the Text Box so that it reaches the edge of the report. The report header should look like Figure 9.19.

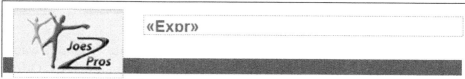

Figure 9.19 The completed report header.

Preview the report to see how it looks.

Working with Indicators

One of the nice things about visual elements is that it allows the busy executive to see how the company is doing at a glance. The executive may even want to see visual data at the detail level. For example, how are each of the company divisions doing and how do they compare to each other? The report can display a number, and also a visual display on each line. In this section, you will learn how to do this with the Indicator control.

The Indicator control allows you to add KPIs to your report. KPI stands for Key Performance Indicator. A KPI is a measure that tells if a specific goal has been met. A KPI might indicate whether the sales people have met their quotas or if a particular retail store has met its sales goals. A KPI is added to a report as a small icon, such as smiley faces, arrows or stop lights. For example, an up arrow means that the value for that row has surpassed the goal. A sideways arrow means that the value is close to the goal and a down arrow means that the value is not even close.

Create a new report called **KPI**. Create a data source based on the shared JProCo data source. Create a dataset called **KPI** based on the query found in the KPI.sql file found at C:\Joes2Pros\SSRSCompanionFiles\Chapter9\Resources. The query contains a list of the sales people along with a total for each year. Using the skills you have learned, add a Table control to the report. Add **FirstName** and **TotalSales** to the report. Group the report by **SalesYear**. The report definition should look like Figure 9.20.

190

Sales Year	First Name	Total Sales	
[SalesYear]			
	[FirstName]	[TotalSales]	

Figure 9.20 The report definition.

From the Toolbox, drag an Indicator control to the cell to the right of **TotalSales**. When you do, the **Select Indicator Type** dialog box (Figure 9.21) opens where you can select the symbol to use in your report. Select one of the groups that has three symbols and click **OK**.

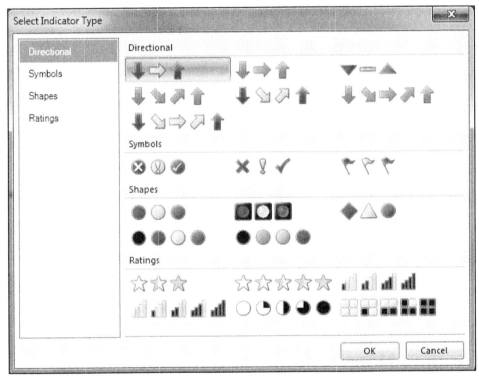

Figure 9.21 The Select Indicator Type dialog box.

Right-click the cell that contains the Indicator and select **Indicator Properties**. Click **Values and States**. In the Value property, select **[Sum([TotalSales])]**. Change the **States Measurement Unit** to **Numeric**.

191

Each symbol must be mapped to a start and end value. For the first icon, set the end value to 20000. Set the start value of the second icon to 20001 and the end value to 60000. Finally, set the start value of the third icon to 60001 and the end value to 100000. The properties should look like Figure 9.22.

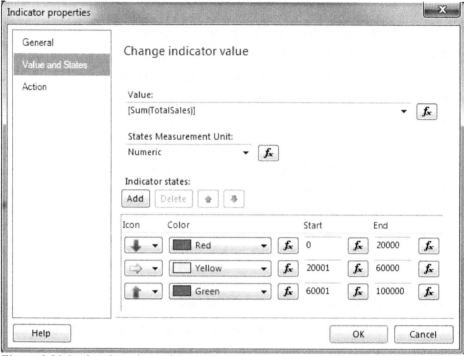

Figure 9.22 Setting the values of the Indicator properties.

Click **OK** and then preview the report. You should see the icon change depending on the value of TotalSales for each employee.

Adding Maps to Reports

The ability to add maps to reports is a very exciting feature of SSRS. Maps can be used to show data represented geographically. A typical use of this feature would be to show which states have the highest sales or which areas have the largest populations. Out of the box, SSRS comes with maps of the United States, but you can also work with ESRI shape files or SQL Server spatial queries. SQL Server has two special data types, geometry and geography, that work well with SSRS maps.

Since this is a beginner book, you will create a simple map that displays the US states and the population per square mile. Begin by creating a new report called **Map**. Add a data source mapped to the shared JProCo data source. Add a dataset called **States** that is based on the query in the Map.sql file found at C:\Joes2Pros\SSRSCompanionFiles\Chapter9\Resources.

From the Toolbox, drag a Map control to the report design canvas. This brings up a wizard to help you configure the map. When asked to **Choose a source of spatial data**, select **Map gallery** and select **USA by State Inset**. Click **Next** twice to reach the **Choose map visualizations** page. Select the **Color Analytical Map** and click **Next**. This type will display different colors depending on the data. Select the **States** dataset and click **Next**. On the next screen you will map your data to the spatial data that came with the map. Uncheck **STATENAME** and check **STUSPS** instead. In the dropdown list, choose **StateId**. This maps the state abbreviations. Click **Next**. On the **Choose color theme and data visualization** page, select **[Sum(PopPerSqMI])]** from the **Field to Visualize** dropdown list and click **Finish**.

Once the wizard completes, click the white area under the legend. This will bring up the **Map Layers** window. Right-click the **PolygonLayer** and choose **Polygon Color Rules**. Figure 9.23 shows how to find this.

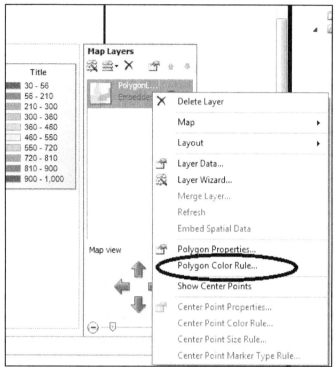

Figure 9.23 The PolygonLayer menu.

Click **Distribution** and change the **Number of subranges** to **20**. This allows a larger number of colors to be used in representing the data. Click **OK** and preview the report. The map should display with highly populated areas in orange or red while sparsely populated areas will display in yellow to green. Figure 9.24 shows the map.

194

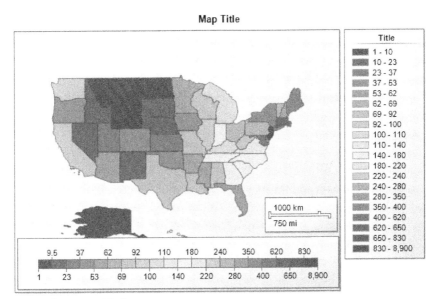

Figure 9.24 The map with data.

Summary

Adding visual elements that convey meaning with just a glance can save your end users lots of time. It is important to note that they are not always appropriate. Be sure to consider your audience and if the visual element actually adds value. Just because you can, doesn't mean you should!

Points to Ponder – Add Visual Appeal

1. Relay information at a glance with visual elements.

2. Drag elements such as charts from the Toolbox to the design canvas.

3. Visual elements such as indicators can also be added to cells.

4. A KPI (Key Performance Indicator) tells at a glance if a target has been reached.

5. Maps can be used to show data geographically.

6. Visual elements and tables can be combined in a report to create a dashboard.

Review Quiz – Chapter Nine

1.) Why would you add visual elements to a report? Select all that apply.

☐ a. To show off your skills.
☐ b. To convey information at a glance.
☐ c. To take up space on the report.
☐ d. To compare two elements, such as this year's sales and last year's sales.

2.) What can be added to reports? Select all that apply.

☐ a. Charts
☐ b. Maps
☐ c. Shapes
☐ d. Indicators

3.) What is a dashboard?

O a. A report composed of more than one section, usually visual elements.
O b. A dashboard is another name for a Tablix report.

Answer Key

1.) The best reasons to use visual elements in a report are (b) and (d).

2.) Charts, maps and indicators may be added to a report. Answer (c) is not correct.

3.) Answer (a) is correct.

[NOTES]

Chapter 10.   Deploying Your Reports

Time and technology have changed many things. One area that is really feeling the effects of technology is the news industry. Having only been part of a small monthly newspaper while in college, I probably have an insignificant understanding of how it really works. I do know that journalists research and write articles that, hopefully, end up being read by the subscribers.

Nowadays, newspapers and magazines are going digital. Regardless of where the articles are published, in print or online, they must be published for readers to have access to them. SSRS is no different. Creating a report does not get the report in the hands of the person who needs it. It must be printed out or published. In this chapter you will learn how to publish SSRS reports to Reporting Services Report Manager.

Discover Report Manager

Reporting Services comes with Report Manager, a web site for publishing and managing reports. With Report Manager, end users can run and print reports whenever they wish. Reports can be organized by folders much like folders or directories on Windows.

READER NOTE: *Reporting Services can also be integrated with SharePoint, which is beyond the scope of this book.*

To get started, you must figure out the URL or path to the Report Manager web site. In this chapter, it is assumed that you'll learn to publish reports within your development environment. To find the URL, go to **Start > All Programs > Microsoft SQL Server 2012 > Configuration Tools > Reporting Services Configuration Manager**. When prompted, click **Connect**. After connecting, click **Report Manger URL**. You will see a hyperlink as shown in Figure 10.1. If you are not able to get to this point, it is possible that you need to configure or install SSRS. Go back to Chapter 2 to learn more.

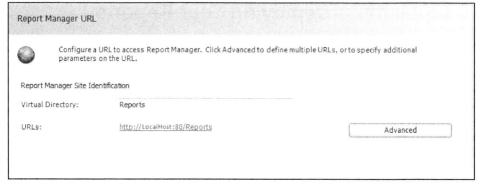

Figure 10.1 The Report Manger URL.

Even though the URL is a hyperlink, don't click it. Because of security features of Windows, you must run the browser as an administrator. Instead, locate your shortcut to Internet Explorer (IE) and while holding down the **SHIFT** key, right-click the **shortcut**. Click **Run as administrator** to launch IE.

Once IE is launched, type in the URL found in the **Reporting Services Configuration Manger** and press **Enter**. Report Manager should launch and look like Figure 10.2.

Figure 10.2 SSRS Report Manager.

Folders

The reports and components are organized within folders. Just like projects in SSDT, you should think about your strategy to avoid creating a mess that is difficult to manage. Click **New Folder** and then click **OK**. There are two views in Report Manager, Tile view and Details view. You can toggle between these two views with the icon on the far right. Figure 10.3 shows Tile view and Figure 10.4 shows Details view.

Figure 10.3 Tile view.

Figure 10.4 Details view.

Details view is helpful for managing SSRS, while Tile view is what your end users will generally see. In each view, by clicking the folder name, you navigate to the folder. If you need to manage the folder, for example to hide it, hover the mouse over the shortcut to see a dropdown menu, as shown in Figure 10.5.

Figure 10.5 Manage the folder.

Click **Manage**. Now you can modify the folder name, add a description or hide the folder. After making a change, click **Apply** to save it. To get back to the **Home** folder, click the **Home** link in the upper left.

Folders can be nested within other folders. You can move and delete folders from the Details view or the menu. You can also set security on the folders in order to control who runs the reports. Security is covered later in the chapter in the Controlling Who Can Run Reports section.

Deploying the Reports in a Project

The easiest way to deploy, or publish, the reports is through SSDT. Within SSDT you can deploy one report at a time or an entire project at once. Because of the security in Windows, if you are deploying reports to your local system you must launch SSDT as an administrator. Close SSDT if it is open. Navigate to the shortcut, hold down the **SHIFT** key and select **Run as administrator**. Open up the **Visual** project you created in Chapter 9. If you did not create the project, you can find it in the Solutions folder for Chapter 9.

In the Solutions Explorer, right-click on the project. Select **Properties**. Expand **Deployment** if it is not already expanded. Everything is filled in for you except for the **TargetServerURL** property. The property can be found in the **Reporting Services Configuration Manager** on the **Web Service URL** page. This is not the same link you used to get to the Report Manager. Most likely it is very close, with **ReportServer** replacing **Reports** in the URL. Figure 10.6 shows my configuration.

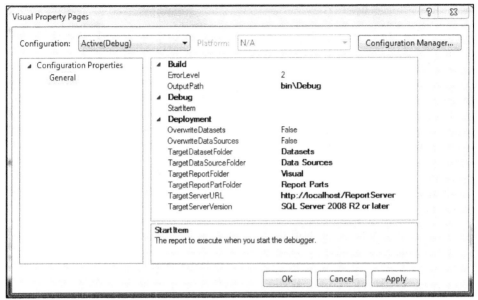

Figure 10.6 The project properties.

Click **OK** after filling in the **TargetServerURL** property. Now you are ready to deploy all the reports in the project. Right-click on the project name and select **Deploy**, as shown in Figure 10.7.

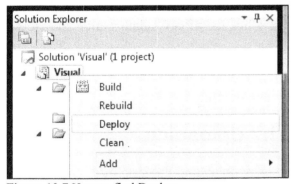

Figure 10.7 How to find Deploy.

While deploying, the Output window should display with the progress. Figure 10.8 shows my results.

203

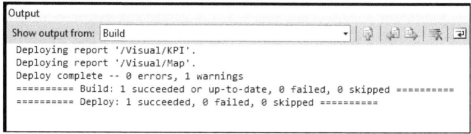

Figure 10.8 The deployment results.

If Report Manager is still shown in your browser, refresh the page. If not, launch it as an administrator. You should now see two new folders, **Data Sources** and **Visual**. Click **Visual** where you will find several report items. Click **Dashboard** and the Dashboard report you created in Chapter 9 should display.

At the very top left, you will see a set of breadcrumb links where you can navigate back to **Home** or to the **Visual** folder. Click **Home**, then click **Data Sources**. You will then see the JProCo shared data source. Shared data sources may be used for many reports, not just the reports from the project where the data source was originally created. If the database server is upgraded and given a new name, you only have to change the name in one place. If the reports have embedded data sources, you have to update each one when there is a change. Click the **JProCo** data source and view the properties.

If you make a change to one report, you can deploy just the one report from SSDT by right-clicking it and selecting **Deploy**.

Deploying a Report by Uploading

Another way to deploy a report is by uploading the report definition file while working in Report Manager. Navigate back to the **Visual** folder and delete the **Dashboard** report, as shown in Figure 10.9.

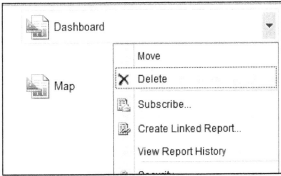

Figure 10.9 Delete the Dashboard report.

When asked if you are sure, click **OK**. Click **Upload File** and then click **Browse**. Navigate to the project files and select the Dashboard.rdl file as shown in Figure 10.10.

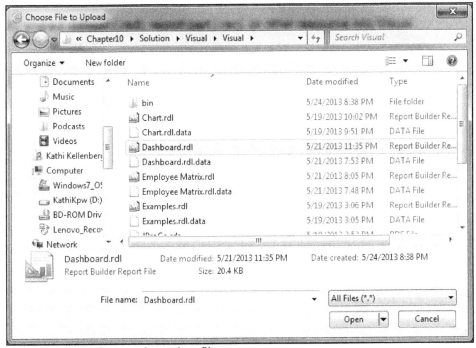

Figure 10.10 Navigate to the project files.

Click **Open** and then click **OK**. The Dashboard report should now be back in place. Unfortunately, if you try to run it, you will get an error about the data source. You will learn how to fix this problem in the next section.

Configuring a Deployed Report

There are many properties you can configure once a report is published. To see all the property categories, hover the cursor over the Dashboard report and select **Manage** from the dropdown menu. Figure 10.11 shows the possible categories.

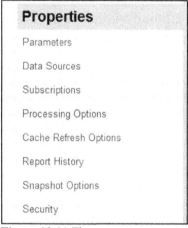

Figure 10.11 The report property categories.

Click **Data Sources** and you will see the error shown in Figure 10.12.

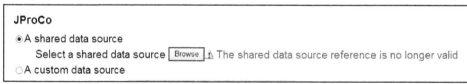

Figure 10.12 The data source error.

Click the **Browse** button and navigate to the **JProCo** data source. Figure 10.13 shows how to find it.

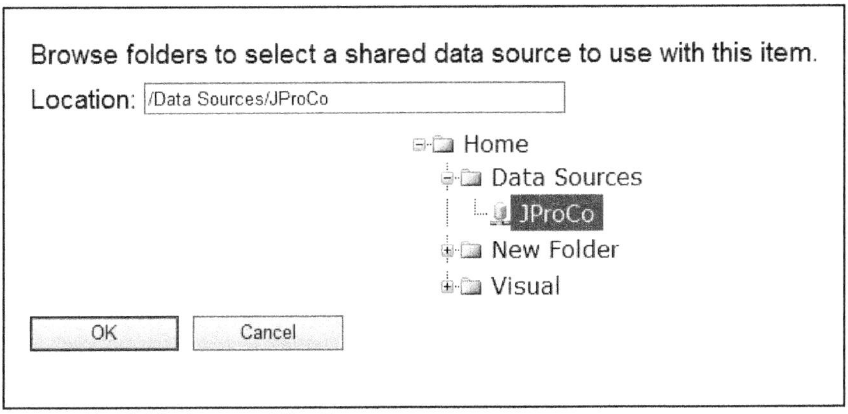

Browse folders to select a shared data source to use with this item.

Location: /Data Sources/JProCo

- ⊟ Home
  - ⊕ Data Sources
    - JProCo
  - ⊕ New Folder
  - ⊕ Visual

[OK]   [Cancel]

Figure 10.13 Navigate to JProCo.

Click **OK** and then click **Apply** once you are back on the **Data Sources** page for the report. Go back to the **Visual** folder by clicking the link at the top of the page and try running the report.

Another very useful set of properties that are often modified is the parameter properties. On the **Manage** menu of the **Dashboard** report, click **Parameters**. Figure 10.14 shows the available properties for the **Year** parameter.

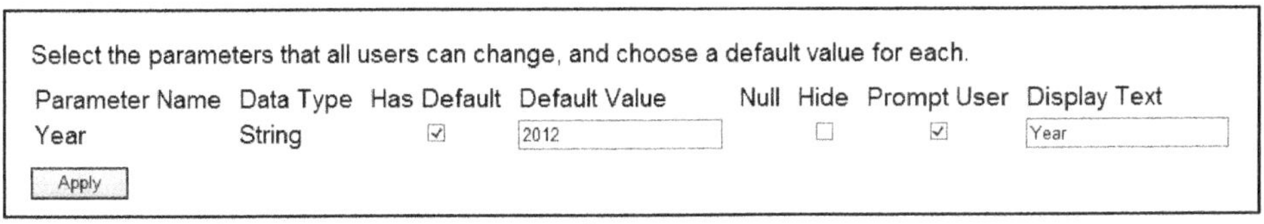

Select the parameters that all users can change, and choose a default value for each.

Parameter Name	Data Type	Has Default	Default Value	Null	Hide	Prompt User	Display Text
Year	String	☑	2012	☐		☑	Year

[Apply]

Figure 10.14 The Year parameter properties.

Change the **Default Value** to **2013** and the **Display Text** to **Enter the Year**. Click **Apply**. Now when you run the report, the parameter will default to 2013 and the prompt will be different.

The other properties are beyond the scope of this book.

Report Builder 3.0

You may have noticed the Report Builder link in the Report Manager menu. Report Builder is a tool meant to allow end users to build their own reports. There are three versions of Report Builder. With SQL Server 2012, you can only use version 3.0. Earlier versions of Report Builder are very different than the 3.0 version and won't be covered in in this book.

If you click the Report Builder link, it will install the tool on your computer. When Report Builder is launched, you will see a screen asking what you wish to do. Figure 10.15 shows the choices.

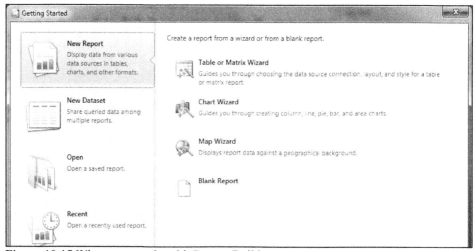

Figure 10.15 What you can do with Report Builder.

Click **New Report** and then **Blank Report**. The Report Builder environment is based on the current Office applications with the ribbon menu. Figure 10.16 shows how the environment looks.

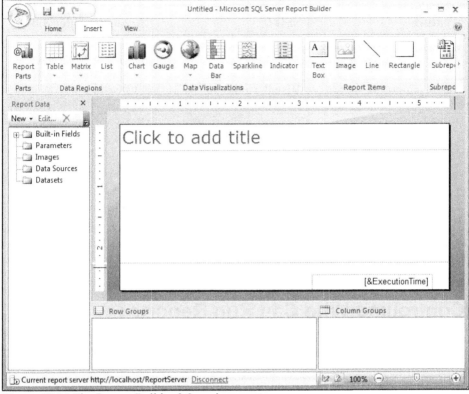

Figure 10.16 The Report Builder 3.0 environment.

You can do just about anything in Report Builder that you can do in SSDT. The skillset is similar, but the menus look very different. Table 10.1 has a list of differences between the two environments.

Table 10.1

Feature	SSDT	Report Builder 3.0
Development model	Professional	End user
Environment	Visual Studio	Office-like
Organization	Projects with multiple reports	Work on one report at a time
SSRS installation	Not required to develop reports	Must be connected to SSRS installation while developing reports
Deployment model	Deploy by menu item or upload	Save

Controlling Who Can Run Reports

The most important part of database professional jobs is security. It is critical that data does not get into the wrong hands. There are two layers of security in place with SSRS. The first layer contains the permissions to view and run reports. The second layer consists of rights to the actual data on the database server.

SSRS uses role-based security to control who can see folders and run reports. You can assign individual accounts or Active Directory groups to the roles. The roles run from powerful administrative rights, the ability to publish reports, down to just the ability to run the reports.

Site Settings

At the site level, there are two default roles: System Administrator and System User. The System Administrator role has powerful rights over the entire site while the System User role has limited rights. The most important reason for using the System User role is to allow the use of the Report Builder tool. You can also create custom roles if required.

To see the site-level security, while in Report Manager, click the **Site Settings** link in the upper right and then click **Security**. Figure 10.17 shows the default rights.

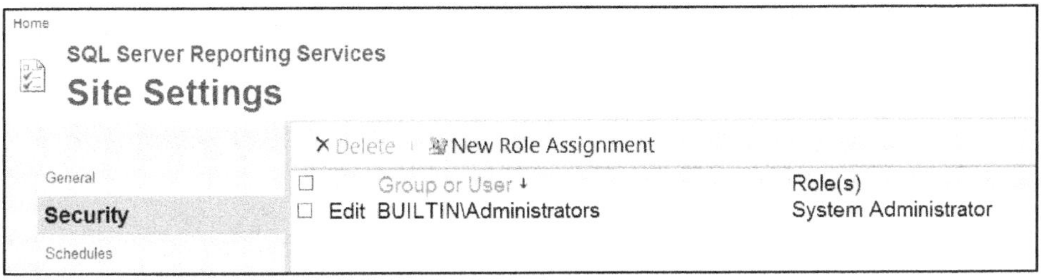

Figure 10.17 Site Settings security.

The BUILTIN\Administrators group has full rights on the computer and within SSRS. To add a new user or group to the System Administrator or System User role click **New Role Assignment**. This brings up the New System Role Assignment screen as shown in Figure 10.18.

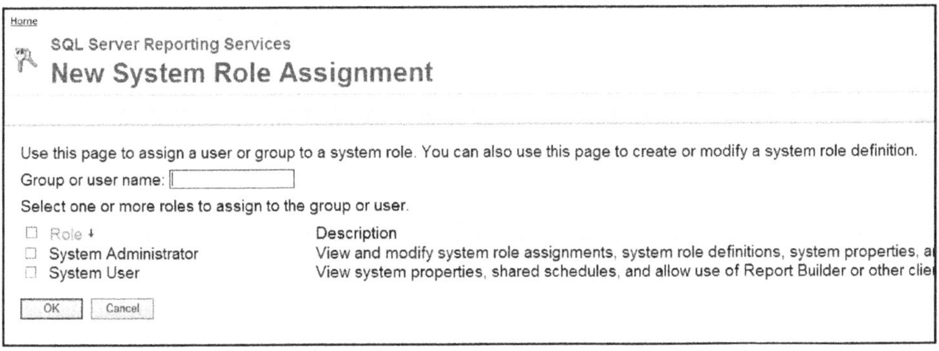

Figure 10.18 New System Role Assignment screen.

To try this out, type **Users** in the **Group or user name** box. Click **System User** and then click **OK**.

To see all of the possible rights at the site level, launch SQL Server Management Studio by holding down the **SHIFT** key, right-clicking the shortcut and selecting **Run as administrator**. When prompted to connect, select **Reporting Services** for the **Server Type** and **Localhost** for the **Server name**. Click **Connect**. Expand **Security** and then **System Roles**.

Double-click **System User** to see the permissions as shown in Figure 10.19.

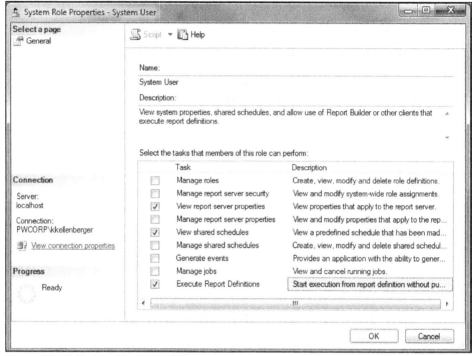

Figure 10.19 System User permissions.

Click **Cancel**. Repeat the process to view the **System Administrator** rights. It is possible to modify the rights of the roles or to create custom roles in SQL Server Management Studio. I suggest that you do not modify the default roles. If there is a special need, create a custom role.

Object-Level Roles

While you will probably not need to make many changes in the site level security, you will modify the object-level security extensively if you create a department or company-wide Reporting Services site. By default, only an administrator on the computer where SSRS is running has rights to view or run the reports. The object-level security has a separate set of roles as shown in Table 10.2.

Table 10.2

Role	Purpose
Browser	The ability to view and run reports
Content Manager	The ability to manage content including publishing reports and resources
My Reports	The ability to publish reports in a special My Reports folder
Publisher	The ability to publish reports
Report Builder	The ability to view report definitions which is required for Report Builder

Just like folders in Windows, SSRS folders and reports inherit rights from parent folders. The ability to override that inheritance enables you to control which users or groups of users can run reports within a folder. As a best practice, only assign rights at the folder level. Do not assign rights to individual reports which could become unmanageable very quickly.

To start out, everyone who might need to run reports should have Browser rights at the Home folder. Then, create folders with specific rights under Home. You can also create subfolders with specific rights. As you can imagine, this strategy takes some planning up front, but will pay off in ease of management in the long run. Just remember, for a user to see a folder and reports, the user must be able to see the parent folder.

In this book, it is assumed that you are running everything on your personal workstation or laptop. In a company, a server will be used to host Report Manager and users will be part of Active Directory. To give you some practice, you will create new groups in your computer that will be given rights.

READER NOTE: *The exercises in this section can only be performed on professional versions of Windows. If you are using a home version of Windows, just read along.*

To get started click the Windows **Start** button, type **Edit local users and groups** in the search box and press **Enter**. This will bring up the **Local Users and Groups** dialog box. Right-click **Groups** and select **New Groups**. Type in **Managers** and click **Create**. The group is created but the dialog box is ready for you to create another group. This time type in **Team Leaders** and click **Create**. Now create a **Team Members** group. Click **Close** to dismiss the dialog box.

Go back to Report Manager and click **Home** if the **Home** folder is not selected. Click **Folder Settings**. By default, the **Builtin\Administrators** has the **Content Manager** role in this and all folders. Click **New Role Assignment**. On the **New Role Assignment** screen type in **Managers** and click **Browser** (Figure 10.20).

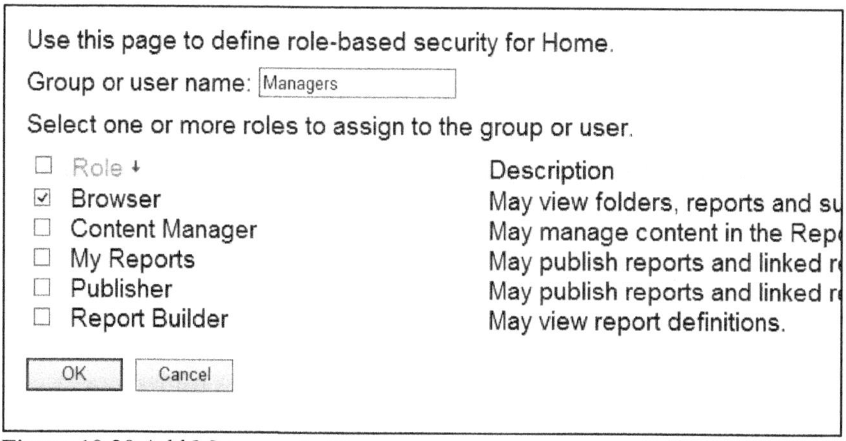

Use this page to define role-based security for Home.

Group or user name: Managers

Select one or more roles to assign to the group or user.

	Role ↓	Description
☐	Browser	May view folders, reports and su
☑	Content Manager	May manage content in the Rep
☐	My Reports	May publish reports and linked r
☐	Publisher	May publish reports and linked r
☐	Report Builder	May view report definitions.

OK   Cancel

Figure 10.20 Add Managers to Home.

Click **OK** and then repeat the process to add the **Team Leaders** and **Team Members** to the Home folder. At this point, the members of all three roles can browse any reports in the site. As you can imagine there are going to be reports that are not meant for the team leaders and members.

Click the **Home** link at the top right to go back to the Home folder. Click **New Folder** to bring up the **New Folder** screen. Type in **Management Reports** and click **OK**. Mouse over the **Management Reports** folder and select **Security** from the dropdown menu. You should see that all three groups have inherited the security from the Home folder, as shown in Figure 10.21.

Edit Item Security	
Group or User ↓	Role(s)
BUILTIN\Administrators	Content Manager
Localhost \Managers	Browser
Localhost \Team Leaders	Browser
Localhost \Team Members	Browser

Figure 10.21 The inherited rights.

Click **Edit Item Security**. When you do, you will be prompted with a warning that you are breaking the inheritance from the parent folder. Click **OK**. Check **Team Members** and click **Delete**. Click **OK** when asked if you want to delete the group. Click **Home** and then click the **Management Reports** folder. Create a new folder under **Management Reports** called **Company Results** and click **OK**. Now remove the **Team Leaders** from this folder.

Now, only managers can view the Company Results folder and any reports found in the folder. Managers and team leaders can see reports in the Management Reports folder. Team members can see any reports at the Home level and the other folders in the site.

Database Security

Managing database security is beyond the scope of this book, but it would be helpful for you to have a basic understanding. Even if a user has rights to run a report, that doesn't mean the user has rights to actually retrieve data from the database. SQL Server security can be set up with Windows accounts and groups or by special SQL Server only accounts.

If the SQL Server instance containing the database for reports happens to be located on the same server as Reporting Services, security is simple. The same groups used to run the report can be used to give rights to the database as well. Unfortunately, if the SQL Server instance with the data is located on a different server, the credentials are not forwarded from the Reporting Server to the database server. This is called the double-hop problem. There is a way to get around this issue by configuring Kerberos security. Kerberos allows the credentials to be passed along to the second server. If you are in need of Kerberos, contact your system administrator for assistance.

The simplest way to configure security at the database level to work with SSRS is to use SQL Server only security. Is this a good idea? Well, it depends on your company rules.

To see how this works, launch SQL Server Management Studio and connect to the Database Engine for the local instance. Make sure that SQL Server allows SQL Server authentication by right-clicking the server name and clicking **Properties**. Click **Security** and make sure that **SQL Server and Windows authentication mode** is selected. If not, you will have to restart SQL Server after changing it. Restart it by right-clicking on the server name and choosing **Restart**.

Once SQL Server is running again, expand the **Security** folder. Right-click the **Logins** folder and select **New Login**. Type in **Report User** for the **Login name**. Select **SQL Server authentication** and type in **pass@word1** for the two password fields. Uncheck **User must change password at next login**. Click **User Mapping** and find the **JProCo** database. Check the **JProCo** database and also check the **db_datareader** role. The screen should look like Figure 10.22.

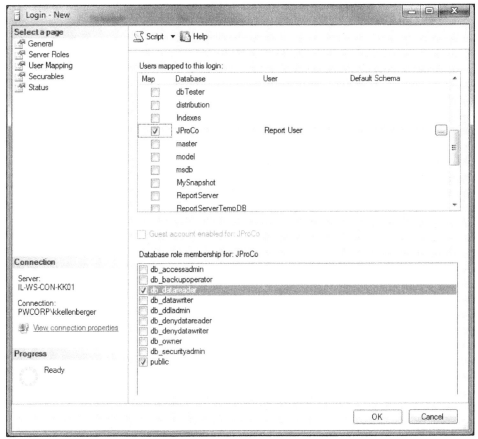

Figure 10.22 The user mapping screen.

Click **OK** to create the account. Now go to the Report Manager and click the **Data Sources** folder. Click the **JProCo** data source to view the properties. Change the **Connect using** property to the **Credentials supplied by the user running the report**. Click **Apply**. Navigate to the **Home > Visual** folder. Click the **Dashboard** report where you will be prompted to enter a user name and password. Enter **Report User** and **pass@word1** to view the report.

You can also store the SQL Server credentials in Reporting Services. Navigate back to the JProCo data source properties and change the **Connect using property** to **Credentials stored securely in report**. Enter

217

Report User as the **User name** and **pass@word1** as the password. Click **Test** connection to make sure the credentials work.

Now when you try running the dashboard, the report will run using the SQL Server account.

Summary

Microsoft has provided a user friendly site for managing and running reports in Report Manager. While it is easy to use, be sure to take time to plan so that the folders are logical and based on the security requirements of your company.

Points to Ponder – Deploy Your Reports

1. Configure the Reporting Services site in the project properties.

2. All the reports in a project can be deployed to Report Manager with just a couple of clicks as long as the destination is configured properly.

3. One report can be deployed by right-clicking the report and choosing Deploy.

4. From Report Manager, you can upload one report at a time.

5. Report properties, such as locating the data source, and modifying the report parameters can be configured in Report Manager.

6. Set security at the folder level, not the report level to make management easier.

7. Add Active Directory user and group accounts to report folders.

8. By default, folders inherit permissions, but you can change that by adding custom permissions on any folder.

9. Report Builder 3.0 is a tool for creating ad-hoc reports. Users can take advantage of pre-built report parts and pre-configured data sets to make building their own reports easy.

Review Quiz – Chapter Ten

1.)   Which statement is true?

   O a.   Item-level security means that you can only configure security at each report item.
   O b.   Reports inherit security from the first report in the folder.
   O c.   You can and should configure security at the folder level.

2.)   How do you deploy the reports in a project?

   O a.   From the Report menu, select Deploy.
   O b.   Right-click on the project and select Deploy.
   O c.   Right-click on Reports and select Deploy.

3.)   Which are the site-wide security roles?

   O a.   Site Administrator and Site User
   O b.   System Administrator and System User
   O c.   Content Manager, Browser, My Reports, Publisher and Report Builder.

Answer Key

1.)   A is not correct because you can configure security at the folder level, not just at the report level. B is not true because reports inherit security from the folder. C is true. You can configure security at the folder level and it is a best practice.

2.)   Answer (b) is correct.

3.)   Answer (b) is correct. Answer (c) is not correct because those are the item-level security roles.

[NOTES]

INDEX

223

CPSIA information can be obtained at www.ICGtesting.com
Printed in the USA
LVOW04s0641200315

431216LV00002B/133/P